PIRKEI AVOT
Jewish Ethical
Ethics of Our Ancestors

Hebrew with English translation

With Commentary
Of The
Rambam
The Mishnah is translated

The commentary of the Rambam
is in English only

There is no known book without mistakes. Therefore, I ask in every language of application if anyone has any questions, comments, clarifications, corrections, please send to: **simchatchaim@yahoo.com**

All material used in this section may not be used for commercial purposes, but only for study and teaching.

To get this book or books and information Email me at:

simchatchaim@yahoo.com

Copyright©All Rights Reserved to

www.simchatchaim.com

Itzhak Aboudi©All rights reserved to the Editor

First Edition 2023

Introduction

Page	Chapter
3.	The Rambam
4.	The Mishnah
7.	PIRKEI AVOT - Jewish Ethical
9.	Chapter 1
26.	Chapter 2
39.	Chapter 3
51.	Chapter 4
71.	Chapter 5
92.	Chapter 6

PIRKI — Small Introduction — Rambam

The Rambam - Rabbi Moses ben Maimon

The Rambam

Rabbi Moses ben Maimon, commonly known as Maimonides, and also referred to by the acronym Rambam, was a medieval Sephardic Jewish philosopher who became one of the most prolific and influential Torah scholars of the Middle Ages. In his time, he was also a preeminent astronomer and physician. Born in Córdoba, Almoravid Empire (present-day Spain) on Passover eve, 1138 (or 1135), he worked as a rabbi, physician, and philosopher in Morocco and Egypt. He died in Egypt on December 12, 1204, whence his body was taken to the lower Galilee and buried in Tiberias.

During his lifetime, most Jews greeted Maimonides' writings on Jewish law and ethics with acclaim and gratitude, even as far away as Iraq and Yemen. Yet, while Maimonides rose to become the revered head of the Jewish community in Egypt, his writings also had vociferous critics, particularly in Spain. Nonetheless, he was posthumously acknowledged as among the foremost rabbinical decisors and philosophers in Jewish history, and his copious work comprises a cornerstone of Jewish scholarship. His fourteen-volume Mishneh Torah still carries significant canonical authority as a codification of Talmudic law. He is sometimes known as "ha'Nesher ha'Gadol" (the great eagle) in recognition of his outstanding status as a bona fide exponent of the Oral Torah.

Aside from being revered by Jewish historians, Maimonides also figures very prominently in the history of Islamic and Arab sciences and is mentioned extensively in studies. Influenced by Al-Farabi, Avicenna, and his contemporary Averroes, he became a prominent philosopher and polymath in both the Jewish and Islamic worlds.

Maimonides composed works of Jewish scholarship, rabbinic law, philosophy, and medical texts. Most of Maimonides's works were written in Judeo-Arabic. However, the Mishneh Torah was written in Hebrew. One of is Jewish texts were **Commentary on the Mishna** (Arabic Kitab al-Siraj, translated into Hebrew as Pirush Hamishnayot), written in Classical Arabic using the Hebrew alphabet. This was the first full commentary ever written on the entire Mishnah, and it enjoyed great popularity both in its Arabic original and its medieval Hebrew translation. The commentary includes three philosophical introductions which were also highly influential:

The Introduction to the Mishnah deals with the nature of the oral law, the distinction between the prophet and the sage, and the organizational structure of the Mishnah.

The Introduction to Mishnah Sanhedrin, chapter ten (Perek Helek), is an eschatological essay that concludes with Maimonides's famous creed ("the thirteen principles of faith").

The Introduction to Tractate Avot (popularly called The Eight Chapters) is an ethical treatise.

The Mishnah

The Mishnah Published at the end of the second century CE, the Mishnah is an edited record of the complex body of material known as oral Torah that was transmitted in the aftermath of the destruction of the Second Temple in 70 CE.

Rabbi Judah the Patriarch, also known as Rabbi Judah the Prince and Yehudah HaNasi, undertook to collect and edit a study edition of these halachot (laws) in order that the learning not vanish.

Although the Temple had been destroyed 130 years prior to its publication, in the world described by the Mishnah the Temple still exists and the laws that governed it are expressed in the present tense. While the Talmud (the compendium of the Mishnah and the Gemara, which interprets and comments on the Mishnah) refers to the Bar Kochba rebellion and the defeat by the Romans, the Mishnah itself ignores the events of the Roman occupation of the land of Israel. In this way, the Mishnah is a document that describes a life of sanctification, in which the rituals of the Temple are adapted for communal participation in a world that has no Temple, which escapes the ups and downs of history.

This idyllic world of the Mishnah, however, is not a world of uniformity; far from it. Most passages in the Mishnah contain a dispute between different rabbinic sages. When does one begin the morning prayers? How does one treat produce that may or may not have had the priestly gifts separated from it? How does one constitute a Jewish marriage? What are the limitations of the liability of someone who watches another's property? Can cheese and meat be on the same table? How much drawn water invalidates a ritual bath? On all of these issues and on thousands of similar issues, the Mishnah includes various opinions.

PIRKI — Small Introduction — Rambam

This is because the Mishnah is not a code of Jewish law; it is a study book of law. As the Mishnah itself describes, in a rare self-reflective comment: Why are the opinions of the minority included with the opinions of the majority even though the law is not like them? So that a later court can examine their words and rely upon them? (Mishnah Eduyot 1:3). While one could determine law based upon the Mishnah, its intention was to train the sages in thinking through the legal issues that inform the halacha (Jewish law).

In editing the Mishnah, Rabbi Judah the Patriarch worked with a variety of materials. Some halachot (laws) of the Tannaim, the sages from the time of the Mishnah, had been transmitted to him organized around a particular sage, some around particular verses, and others according to certain formal characteristics. Signs of these pre-existing collections are still apparent in the Mishnah. On the other hand, it is also clear that Rabbi Judah was not simply a collector. He selected his sources from a larger pool of available material, and he modified his sources, combining and editing materials to facilitate memorization and to clarify the points of dispute between the different sages.

The Mishnah is divided into six orders; each order is divided into tractates; each tractate is divided into chapters, and each chapter has a number of halachot. This structure became the template for all subsequent Talmud ic literature. The first document to follow the Mishnah's structure was the Tosefta (supplement), which included many of the materials that Rabbi Judah left out. Collectively, the Tosefta, as well as materials in works of Midrash (biblical interpretation), and materials preserved orally until their appearance in the

Talmud are called Baraitot (excluded materials). The terms Tosefta and Baraitot, which implicitly refer to the Mishnah, serve to emphasize the significance and centrality of the Mishnah in Jewish culture.

PIRKEI AVOT
Ethics of Our Ancestors - Jewish Ethical

Atop Mount Sinai, over the course of forty days and nights, G-d taught Moses the entire Torah. The Torah was a two-part study: the "Written Torah," transcribed in the Five Books of Moses (and later extended to include all the 24 books of the Scriptures), and the "Oral Torah," a commentary on the Written Torah. The Oral Torah was orally transmitted from teacher to student for many generations. In the 2nd century CE, Rabbi Judah the Prince felt that the Oral Law would be forgotten unless it was transcribed. So, he compiled the basics into a six-part document called the Mishnah.Pirkei Avot, also spelled as Pirkei Avoth or Pirkei Avos or Pirke Aboth, which translates to English as Chapters of the Fathers, is a compilation of the ethical teachings and maxims from Rabbinical Jewish tradition. It is part of didactic Jewish ethical literature. Because of its contents, the name is sometimes given as Ethics of the Fathers. Pirkei Avot consists of the Mishnaic tractate of Avot, plus one additional chapter. Avot is unique in that it is the only tractate of the Mishnah dealing solely with ethical and moral principles; there is little or no halacha (laws) found in Pirkei Avot.The Mishnaic tractate Avot consists of five chapters. It begins with an order of transmission of the Oral Tradition; Moses receives the Torah at Mount

PIRKI — Small Introduction — Rambam

Sinai and then transmits it through various generations (including Joshua, the Elders, and the Neviim, but notably not the Kohanim), whence it finally arrives at the Great Assembly, i.e., the Rabbis (Avot 1:1). It contains sayings attributed to sages from Simon the Just (200 BCE) to shortly after Judah haNasi (200 CE), redactor of the Mishnah. These aphorisms concern proper ethical and social conduct, as well as the importance of Torah study.

PIRKI AVOT — Chapter 1 — Rambam

Chapter 1

1. Moses[1] received the Torah at Sinai and transmitted it to Joshua, Joshua to the elders, and the elders to the prophets, and the prophets to the Men of the Great Assembly. They said three things: Be[2] patient in [the administration of] justice, raise many disciples, and[3] make a fence round the Torah.

2. Shimon the Righteous was one of the last of the men of the great assembly. He used to say[4]: the world stands

---

[1] **Rambam** - We have already explained the description of how the transmission happened in the introduction of our words in this essay. And so, our intention here is only to explain the words of piety and ethics alone, to encourage the acquisition of certain virtues the benefit from which is great. And we will also elaborate to warn about certain vices that [bring] much damage. And [for] the rest, I will only explain the words and some of the concepts, because their concepts are [already] clear, except for a few of them.

[2] **Rambam** - Be deliberate in judgment: That they should delay in reaching the verdict and not determine it quickly before they [fully] understand it. As it is possible that new matters will be revealed to their eyes that were not revealed at the beginning of [their] thought.

[3] and make a fence for the Torah: they mean to say the decrees and ordinances that distance a man from sins. As He, may He be blessed stated (Leviticus 18:30), "And you shall guard My guarding." And it was said in its explanation, "Make a guarding [fence] for My guarding."

[4] **Rambam** - He is saying that with wisdom, and that is the Torah; and with enhancement of [good] traits, and that is acts of lovingkindness; and with the fulfillment of commandments, and that is the sacrifices [referred to in the mishnah as service] - there

PIRKI AVOT   Chapter 1   Rambam

upon three things: the Torah, the Temple service, and the practice of acts of piety.

3. Antigonus a man of Socho received the oral tradition from Shimon the Righteous. He used to say[5]: do not be

---

will be a continuous refinement of the world and ordering of its existence in the most complete way.

[5] **Rambam** - A reward (pras) is what one calls a benefit that is granted to a person by someone who does not gain from him, but [rather] does it by way of kindness and grace. [It is] like when a man tells his servant or his young son or his wife, "Do such and such and I will give you a dinar or two." That is the difference between a reward and a wage (sachar), since a wage is that which is given by [way of an] obligation. And this pious one said that you should not serve God, may He be blessed, in order that He will do good to you and benefit you with kindness and that you should hope for the benefit and serve Him for its sake. Indeed, serve Him like servants that are not hoping for endowment or the giving of kindness. He meant with this that they should serve Him from love, as we said in Chapter Ten of Sanhedrin. And nonetheless, he did not exempt us from fear [of God]. And [so] he said, "Even as you serve from love, do not discard fear completely, 'and may the fear of Heaven be upon you.'" As the commandment of fear has already come in the Torah, and that is its stating (Deuteronomy 6:13), "Fear the Lord, your God." And the sages said (Yerushalmi Berakhot 9:7), "Serve from love, serve from fear," and they said that the one who loves will not forget a thing from that which he was commanded to do, and the one who fears will not do what he was warned from doing - as fear is a great pathway with the negative commandments, and all the more so, with the arational commandments. And this sage had two students - one whose name was Tsadok and one whose name was Beitos. And when they heard him say this statement, they went out from in front of him and one said to his fellow, "Behold, the teacher said explicitly that there is no benefit and punishment for a person and there is no hope at all" - as they did not understand his intention. And one strengthened the hand of

PIRKI AVOT   Chapter 1   Rambam

like servants who serve the master in the expectation of receiving a reward, but be like servants who serve the master without the expectation of receiving a reward, and let the fear of Heaven be upon you.

4. Yose ben Yoezer a man of Zeredah and Yose ben Yohanan a man of Jerusalem received the oral tradition

---

his friend and they exited the group and left the Torah. One group connected itself to one and another group to his fellow. And the sages called them Sadducees and Boethusians. But when they could not gather congregations due to that which follows from this belief - as this evil belief disengages the united, all the more so will it not unite the disengaged - they leaned towards belief in the thing which they could not deny among the masses. As if they would put this out of their mouths, [the masses] would have killed them. I mean to say [that this thing is] the words of Torah. And [so] each one said to his party that he believes in the Torah, but disagrees with the transmission [of its oral explanation] - that it is not true. And this was to exempt themselves from the accepted commandments and ordinances and decrees. Since they could not push off everything - the written [Torah] and the received [explanation]. And also [this way], the way of interpretation was broadened for them. Since once the explanation was given to their choice, he was able to be lenient in what he wanted and to be strict in what he wanted. [This is] since he did not believe in the fundamentals at all, yet he sought things that would still be accepted by some people. And these evil groups came out from then. And they are called Karaites in these lands - I mean to say, Egypt. And their names among the sages are Sadducees and Boethusians. And they are the ones that began to question the transmission and to explain all of the verse according to what appears to them without listening to the sage at all, [which is] the opposite of what He, may He be blessed, stated (Deuteronomy 17:11), "You shall act in accordance with the instructions given you and the ruling handed down to you; you must not deviate from the verdict that they announce to you either to the right or to the left."

PIRKI AVOT — Chapter 1 — Rambam

from them [i.e. Shimon the Righteous and Antigonus]. Yose ben Yoezer used to say[6]: let thy house be a house of meeting for the Sages, and sit in the very dust of their feet, and drink in their words with thirst.

5. Yose ben Yochanan a man of Jerusalem used to say: Let thy house be wide open[7], and let the poor[8] be members of thy household. Engage not in too much conversation with women. They[9] said this with regard to one's own wife, how much more, does the rule apply with regard to another man's wife. From here the Sages said: as long as a man engages in too much conversation with women, he causes evil to himself,

---

[6] **Rambam** - "A meeting house": A house of meeting, meaning to say that you should make your house always available for the gathering of sages, like in synagogues and houses of study (batei midrash); such that if a man says to his fellow, "Where can I meet with you, where can I confer with you," he will [answer] him, "In the house of one."

[7] **Rambam** - "Open": That you should have a gate open to the path of wayfarers, such that every wayfarer that need something or is hungry or thirsty will enter the house immediately.

[8] **Rambam** - "may the poor be members of your household": He is saying that it is necessary that the servants be the poor and the indigent. And this is more fit than purchasing slaves. And so would the sages condemn the purchase of slaves and praise one whose servants and members of his household were the poor.

[9] **Rambam** - They so stated with his wife: It is known that the majority of talk with women is about matters of sex. Because of this, he said that increasing conversation with them is forbidden, since he "causes evil to himself." He means to say that he acquires lowly traits for his soul, and that is the abundance of desire.

he[10] neglects the study of the Torah, and in the end, he[11] will inherit gehinnom.

6. Joshua ben Perahiah and Nittai the Arbelite received the oral tradition from them. Joshua ben Perahiah used to say: appoint[12], for thyself a teacher, and acquire for

---

[10] **Rambam** - "and neglects the words of Torah": It is understood that he wastes time with other occupations.

[11] **Rambam** - "and, in his end, he inherits Geihinam": because of this conversation of rebellion, and he obligates himself in the punishment.

[12] **Rambam** - "Make for yourself a mentor": He means to say even if he is not fit to be your mentor; still place him upon you as a mentor, so that you can give and take (discuss and argue) with him, and as a result of this the study of wisdom will come to your hand. As the study of a man on his own is good, but his study from someone else will be better established in his hand and it will be more clear - and even if he is like him in wisdom or below him. And so did they elucidate the explanation of this commandment. And he said, "acquire for yourself a friend". He said it with an expression of acquisition and he did not say, "Make for yourself a friend," or "Befriend others." The intention of this is that a person must acquire a friend for himself, so that all of his deeds and all of his matters be refined through him, as they said (Taanit 23a), "Either a friend or death." And if he does not find him, he must make efforts for it with all his heart, and even if he must lead him to his friendship, until he becomes a friend. And [then] he must never let off from following [his friend's] will, until his friendship is firmed up. [It is] as the masters of ethics say, "When you love, do not love according to your traits; but rather love according to the trait of your friend." And when each of the friends has the intention to fulfill the will of his friend, the intention of both of them will be one without a doubt. And how good is the statement of Aristotle, "The friend is one." And there are three types of friends: a friend for benefit, a friend for enjoyment and a friend for virtue. Indeed, a friend for benefit is like the friendship of two [business] partners and

thyself a companion, and[13] judge all men with the scale weighted in his favor.

---

the friendship of a king and his retinue; whereas the friendship for enjoyment is of two types - the friend for pleasure and the friend for confidence. Indeed, the friend for pleasure is like the friendship of males and females and similar to it; whereas the friend for confidence is when a man has a friend to whom he can confide his soul. He will not keep [anything] from him - not in action and not in speech. And he will make him know all of his affairs - the good ones and the disgraceful - without fearing from him that any loss will come to him with all of this, not from him and not from another. As when a person has such a level of confidence in a man, he finds great enjoyment in his words and in his great friendship. And a friend for virtue is when the desire of both of them and their intention is for one thing, and that is the good. And each one wants to be helped by his friend in reaching this good for both of them together. And this is the friend which he commanded to acquire; and it is like the love of the master for the student and of the student for the master.

[13] **Rambam** - "and judge every person as meritorious:" Its subject is when there is a person whom you do not about him if he is righteous or if he is wicked and you see him doing an act or saying something and if you interpret it one way it will be good and if you interpret in another way it will be bad - [in this case,] take it to the good and do not think bad about it. But if the man is known to be famously righteous and of good deeds; and an action of his is seen that all of its aspects indicate that it is a bad deed and a person can only determine it to be good with great stretching and a distant possibility, it is fit that you take it that it is good, since there is some aspect of a possibility that it is good. And it is not permissible for you to suspect him; and about this did they say (Shabbat 97a), "The body of anyone who suspects proper ones will be struck." And so [too] when it is an evildoer and his deeds are famous, and afterwards we see him that he does a deed, all of the indications about which are that it is good but there is an aspect of a distant possibility that it is bad; it is fit to guard oneself from him and not to believe that it is good, since

PIRKI AVOT   Chapter 1   Rambam

7. Nittai the Arbelite used to say: keep a distance from an evil neighbor, do[14] not become attached to the wicked, and do not abandon faith in [divine] retribution.

8. Judah ben Tabbai and Shimon ben Shetach received the oral tradition from them. Judah ben Tabbai said: do[15] not as a judge play the part of an advocate; and when

---

there is a possibility for the bad. And about this is it stated (Proverbs 26:25), (Also) "Though he be fair-spoken do not trust him, etc." But when he is not known and the deed is indeterminate towards one of the two extremes; according to the ways of piety, one must judge a person as meritorious towards whichever extreme of the two extremes [would be the case].

[14] **Rambam** - "Do not befriend an evildoer": in any type of friendship and companionship, so that you will not learn from his deeds. And we have already elucidated in the previous chapters that a man learns from the vices [found] in the company of evildoers. And he said [further] if you sin or you see that one sin, do not be confident and say that God, may He be blessed, will only punish him in the world to come; and do not despair of quick vengeance from Him for this sin.

[15] **Rambam** - "The judges' advisers (literally, organizers)": They are people that study the arguments and the laws until the people become experts in their cases. As they compose questions and answers: when the judge says this, answer him that; and when the litigant argues this, so should be your answer - as if they are organizing the case, and the litigant is [coming] in front of them. And that is why they are called the judges' organizers - it is as if they organize the cases in front of them. And they warned them from being similar to them; meaning to say to teach one of the litigants an argument that will benefit him and to say to him, "Say this," or "Refute [an opposing claim] in such and such a way." And even if he knew about him that he was the victim and that his fellow's claim against him is false according to what he truly thinks, nonetheless, it is not permissible for him to teach him an argument that will save him or benefit him at all.

the litigants are standing before you, look upon them as if they were both guilty; and when they leave your presence, look upon them as if they were both innocent, when they have accepted the judgement.

9. Shimon ben Shetach used to say: be thorough in the interrogation of witnesses, and be careful with your words, lest from them they learn to lie.

10. Shemaiah and Abtalion received the oral tradition from them. Shemaiah used to say: love work, hate acting the superior, and[16] do not attempt to draw near to the ruling authority.

11. Abtalion used to say: Sages be careful with your words, lest you incur the penalty of exile, and be carried off to a place of evil[17] waters, and the disciples who

---

[16] **Rambam** - This 'government' (rishut) is the authorities. And in these three traits there is refinement of faithfulness and of the world. As with the absence of work, things will be tight for him and he will rob and be unfaithful. And with the pursuit of lordship, he will have challenges in the world and bad things; as since people will be jealous of him and disagree with him, he will lose his faithfulness. [It is] as they said (Sanhedrin 103b), "Once a man is appointed an officer over the community below, he becomes an evildoer above." And so [too, regarding] familiarity with the government in the early days and coming close to it, it was very unusual to escape from [the damage caused by] it in this world. As he will not pay attention to anything except that which brings him close to it. And you know the matter with Doeg - and even though the authority with which Doeg became close was the anointed of God and a prophet and God's chosen one, may He be blessed.

[17] **Rambam** - "Evil waters" is a nickname for heresy. And they said, "Be careful with your words" among the masses, and there should not be in in your words [something] that can support a different interpretation [than what you mean]. As if there are heretical men there, they will interpret them according to their

PIRKI AVOT   Chapter 1   Rambam

follow you drink and die, and thus the name of heaven becomes profaned.

12. Hillel and Shammai received the oral tradition from them. Hillel used to say: be[18] of the disciples of Aaron,

---

beliefs. And the students will have already heard them from them and they will turn to heresy. And they will think that these were your beliefs and there will be a desecration of God, as happened to Antigonos with Tsadok and Beitos.

[18] **Rambam** - "Of the disciples of Aharon": They said (The Fathers According to Rabbi Nathan 12) that when Aharon, peace be upon him, sensed that the insides of a person were bad or they told him that his insides were bad or that he had a sin in his hand, he would greet him first and would be friendly towards him and would speak much with him. And that man would become embarrassed about himself and say, "Woe is to me! If Aharon knew what is hidden in my heart and the evil of my actions, he would not permit himself to [even] look at me, all the more so to speak to me. And yet he treats me with the presumption that I am a proper man. [Hence] I will confirm his words and his thought and I will return to the good." And he would become from his students who learn from him. And the Holy One, blessed be He, stated when He described him with this trait (Malachi 2:6), "He walked with Me in peace and righteousness, and brought many backs from iniquity." And it is this famous matter about him that Hillel had in mind. And he also said when a man's name spreads for greatness, its termination will be announced. And he would also say, that God, may He be blessed, kills the one who doesn't read [the Bible] much, but the one who does not learn at all is fitting to be killed [now]. And [he also said] that one who "uses the crown" will die, meaning to say one who earns a livelihood from Torah and receives [tangible] benefit from it. And this was his intention in this statement, as will be explained in this tractate (Rambam on Pirkei Avot 4:5). And it is stated by way of mnemonic, "Student (yes), another man (no)," meaning to say that it is not permissible for a Torah scholar to receive service from any man except for his students.

loving peace and pursuing peace, loving mankind and drawing them close to the Torah.

13. He also used to say: one who makes his name great causes his name to be destroyed; one who does not add [to his knowledge] causes [it] to cease; one who does not study the Torah deserves death; one who makes unworthy use of the crown of learning shall pass away.

14. He also used to say: If[19] I am not for myself, who is for me? But if I am for my own self only, what am I? And if not now, when?

---

[19] **Rambam** - He said, "If I myself will not be the one that arouses my soul to virtue, who will arouse me, as I have no one to stimulate me from outside," like we have elucidated in the second chapter (Eight Chapters 2). "And since it is in my power to incline my soul to any side that I want, what deed have I done from the good deeds." It is as if he is [questioning] himself and saying, "What am I?" [This is] to say, "What is [becoming of] me? I am not complete, even if I did this matter." And afterwards he went back and said, "If I do not acquire these traits now in the days of my youth, when will I acquire them? Not in the days of old age, as it is difficult to veer from [one's] characteristics at that time because the acquisitions and the traits have hardened and settled - whether they are virtues or whether they are vices." And the wise one said (Proverbs 22:6), "Educate a youth according to his way, and he will also not veer from it when he gets old."

15. Shammai used to say: make[20] your study of the Torah a fixed practice; speak little, but do much; and[21] receive all men with a pleasant countenance.

16. Rabban Gamaliel used to say[22]: appoint for thyself a teacher, avoid doubt, and do not make a habit of tithing by guesswork.

17. Shimon, his son, used to say[23]: all my days I grew up among the sages, and I have found nothing better for

---

[20] **Rambam** - He said to make Torah study the center and the main thing and your other affairs secondary to it - whether they turn up or whether they not turn up, since there is no damage [from their] absence. And they said (Bava Metzia 87a), "The righteous say little and do much" - like our father, Avraham, who designated one loaf of bread and brought "curds and milk and a calf" (Genesis 18:8) and three seah of fine flour. "And evildoers say much and do not do even a little" - like Efron who gave everything [away] in his words, but in practice did not even leave one small coin from the [purchase price].

[21] **Rambam** - "a pleasant countenance": That is when he interacts with the creatures calmly and with pleasant and welcome words.

[22] **Rambam** - Rabban Gamliel says, "Make for yourself a mentor, remove yourself from doubt and do not frequently tithe by estimation." That which he commanded here to make a mentor is not regarding study, but rather legal decisions: place for yourself a mentor, that you can rely upon in the forbidden and the permissible, and you can remove yourself from doubt. [It is] as they say in Talmud Yerushalmi Moed Katan 1:10, "Go and bring me an elder from the marketplace and I will rely upon him and permit [it] to you." And so [too] did he command to flee from putting out tithes by estimation, because it is from the doubts.

[23] **Rambam** - The wise one has already stated (Proverbs 10:19), With many words, there is no lack of transgression." And the reason for this is that most words add superfluity and sin, as I will elucidate now. As when a man increases his words, he will

PIRKI AVOT — Chapter 1 — Rambam

certainly transgress, since it is impossible that there will not be in his words one word that is not fit to say. And one of the signs of the wise is minimization of words, and one of the signs of the foolish is the multitude of words. And the sages have already said that the minimization of words is proof of the high virtue of the forefathers. And when a man was pedigreed, they would say, "The pedigreed one of Babylonia is the quiet one." And it is said in the Book of Characteristics that one of the sages was seen to be silent, since he did not say speech that was not fitting to speak and he only spoke very little. And they said to him, "What is the reason for your great silence?" And he said, "I have examined all speech and I have found it divided into four divisions.

The first division is completely injurious, without benefit, like the cursing of people or vulgarity and similar to them; such that to speak with them is complete idiocy.

And the second division is injurious on one side but beneficial on the other side, like the praise of a man to gain benefit from him. But in that praise will be that which will anger his enemy and so [the speech] will injure the one being praised. And one should refrain from this speech because of this reason, [such] that they not speak things from this division as well.

And the third division is words that have no benefit and no injury like most of the speech of the masses: how was wall one built?; how was hall y built; or the telling of the beauty of house one or the multitude of delicacies of country y; and similar to these. These are extraneous words - one who says such words is excessive and there is no benefit in them.

And the fourth division are words that are completely beneficial, like the speech about the wisdoms and about the virtues and the speech of a person about what is specific to him, in that his life depends upon them and through them will his existence continue. And he must speak this." He said, "Any time I hear words, I examine them. And if I find that they are from this fourth division, I speak them. But if they are from the other divisions, I am silent about them." And the [author] of the [Book of] Characteristics examined this man and his wisdom which is to avoid three-fourths of speech, and [found] that this wisdom is

PIRKI AVOT — Chapter 1 — Rambam

the one that needs to be taught. And I say that speech is divided into five parts according to the Torah's obligation: 1) We are commanded about it; 2) We are warned against it; 3) The disgusting; 4) The beloved; 5) The permissible.

The first division is that which one is commanded about - and it is reading the Torah and studying it and reading its analysis. And this is an obligatory positive commandment, as it is stated (Deuteronomy 6:7), "and you shall speak in them." And it is as weighty as all of the other commandments [put together]. And it has already been said about the imperative of study that which not even a part of would fit in this [entire] composition.

The second division is the speech that is forbidden and that we are warned against, such as false testimony, talebearing and cursing. And the words of the Torah teach about this division. And also [included] are foul speech and evil speech.

And the third division is the disgusting that has no benefit to a man for himself, but is not a sin and not rebellious - like the speech of the masses about what happened and what was and what are the customs of King x in his chamber and how was the cause of y's death or how did z become rich. And the sages call these idle talks; and the pious ones made efforts for themselves to refrain from this division of speech. And it was said about Rav, the student of Rabbi Hiya, that he did not speak idle talk all of his days. And from this division is also when a person disgraces a virtue or praises a vice - whether they be intellectual or dispositional.

And the fourth division is the beloved, and that is speech in praise of intellectual virtues or dispositional virtues and in disgrace of both types of vice - to awaken the soul to the virtues with stories and songs, and to prevent the vices in these same ways. And also to praise the distinguished and to acknowledge their virtues, so that their practices be valued in the eyes of people and that they walk in their ways; and to disgrace the bad about their vices, so that their action and their memory be disgraced in the eyes of people and that they distance themselves from them and not act according to their practices. And this division - meaning to say, study of the virtuous traits and distancing from traits of vice - is called derekh erets (the way of the world).

The fifth division is the permissible and is the speech about what is specific to a person about his business, his livelihood, his food, his drink, his clothing and the rest of what he needs for himself. And it is permissible - it is not beloved or disgusting. Rather, if he wants, he can speak what he wants of it, and if he wants, he will not speak [it]. And with this division, a person is praiseworthy when he minimizes his speaking of it. And the men of ethics have warned about increasing words in it. But the forbidden and the disgusting does not require a warning nor a commandment, as it is fitting to be completely silent from it. However, the commanded and the beloved [speech], if a person could speak in it all of his days, it would be good. However, one must be careful about two things: The one is that his deeds match his words, as they said, "Pleasant are the words that come out of the mouth of one who does them." And about this matter did he intend in his saying, "And the exposition [of Torah] is not what is essential, but the action." And the sages say to a righteous one that [specifically] he teach the virtues, in their saying, "Expound, and for you it is fit to expound." And the prophet stated (Psalms 33a), "Rejoice, righteous ones in the Lord; for the straight is praise beautiful." And the other matter is terseness and that he make efforts to maximize content with few words and not that the matter be the opposite. And this is what they said (Pesachim 3a), "A man should teach his students in the brief way." And know that songs, that are composed in any language that it be, must be examined for their contents - if they are following the way of speech that we have divided. And indeed, I have clarified this even though it is clear [already], because I have seen elders and and pious men from the people of our Torah when they are at a wine party like a wedding or something else and a person wants to sing an Arabic song - even if the subject of that song is praise of courage or generosity and that is from the division of the beloved, [as well as] when it is in praise of wine - they push it off with every angle of distancing, and it is not permissible according to them to hear it. And when the lyricist sings one of the Hebrew canticles it is not bad in their eyes if it is from the things that we are warned against or which are disgusting. And this is complete foolishness, as speech is not forbidden or extraneous or beloved or disgusting or commanded in its saying because of the language that it is in, but rather because of its content. As if the content of that song is virtue, he is obligated to say it - in any language that it my be. But if the intention of that song is vice in any language that it should be, it is forbidden to say it [- in any language that it should be]. I also have what to add to this: When there are two canticles and they express the same content of arousing the power of desire and praise for it and to rejoice the soul with it - and it is vice and it is from the division of disgusting speech since it enthuses and arouses a trait of vice, as is clarified in our words in the fourth chapter - but one of the two canticles is in Hebrew and one is in Arabic or vernacular; listening to the Hebrew and speaking it is more disgusting to the Torah due to the level of the language, as it is only right to use it for virtues. All the more so if they require to put into it a verse from the Torah or from the Song of Songs about that matter - as then, it goes from the division of the disgusting to the division of the forbidden and what is warned against. As the Torah forbade to make the words of prophecy types of song for vice and disgusting things. And since we have mentioned evil speech in the division of forbidden speech, I saw [fit] to elucidate it and to mention a little of what is mentioned about it. As people are in great blindness about it and it is the great sin that is always in people - and all the more so about what the sages said (Bava Batra 164b) that a person does not escape from tangential evil speech on any day. And who would give that we escape from evil speech itself! And evil speech is the recounting of the evils of a man and his blemishes and the disgracing of a man of Israel in whatever side of disgrace that it be - and even if the disgraced was lacking as was spoken. As evil speech is not that he lies about a man and attribute to him that which he does not do, as that is called putting out a bad name on his fellow. However evil speech is that when he disgraces the disgraces of a person, even about his actions that he truly does,

PIRKI AVOT — Chapter 1 — Rambam

[such] that the speaker sins and the one who hears him sins. They said (Arakhin 15b), "There are three that evil speech kills: the one who speaks it, the one who listens to it and the one they are speaking about." And they said, "The one who listens to it more than the one who speaks it." And tangential evil speech is the mention of the blemishes of a man without clarification. Shlomo said about this matter that sometimes one who mentions the blemishes of a person without clarification shows that he does not have knowledge of that which is understood from his words and that he did not intend this, but rather intended another matter - as he said (Proverbs 26:18-19), "Like a madman scattering deadly firebrands, arrows, is one who cheats his fellow and says, 'I was only joking.'" And one of the sages from among the wise ones already praised in a large group the writing of a scribe that he showed him; and the rabbi condemned the act of the praiser and said (Mishnah Arakhin 3:5), "Go and stop your evil speech." [He meant] to say that you are causing his disgrace with your praise of him in the large group. As from them is one who loves him and one who hates him, and his enemy will be forced to mention his blemishes and his evils when he hears his praises. And that is an extreme distancing from evil speech. And the language of the Mishnah (Mishnah Arakhin 3:5) is "the judgment against our ancestors in the wilderness was sealed only because of their evil speech" - meaning to say the matter of the scouts about which it was stated (Numbers 13:32), "And they put out slander of the land." And they, peace be upon them, said (Arakhin 15a), "And if these that only put out a bad name on trees and stones become liable for what they became liable, how much more is it so for someone who speaks about the disgrace of his fellow!" And this is the language of the Tosefta (Talmud Yerushalmi Peah 1:1): For three sins is there retribution to a person in this world and he does not have a share in the world to come - idolatry, sexual immorality and murder; and evil speech corresponds to all of them [together]. And they said in the Gemara (Arakhin 15b) [that] with idolatry comes the expression, 'the big' - and that is its stating (Exodus 32:31), "Alas, this people is guilty of a big sin." And with the sin of sexual immorality also

a person than silence. Study is not the most important thing, but actions; whoever indulges in too many words brings about sin.

18. Rabban Shimon ben Gamaliel used to say[24]: on three things does the world stand: On justice, on truth and on peace, as it is said[25]: "execute the judgment of truth and peace in your gates".

---

comes the expression, 'the big' - and that is its stating (Genesis 39:9), "and how can I do the big evil, this one." And with the sin of murder also comes the expression, 'the big' - and that is its stating (Genesis 4:13), "Is my sin too big to carry?" But with evil speech comes the expression 'the big ones' (plural)." [It] means to say that it corresponds to the three of them [together] - and that is its stating (Psalms 12:4) "tongue speaking big things.'" And they spoke about this unsettling sin very much. And the end of that which is said is that "Anyone who speaks evil speech denies the fundamental [faith], as it is stated (Psalms 12:5), 'They say, "By our tongues we shall prevail; with lips such as ours, who can be our master?"'" Indeed, I have said a little of what they said about this sin; even though I have written at length, in order that a man distance himself from it with all of his ability and make his intention to be quiet - meaning to say from this division of speech.

[24] **Rambam** - Judgement is the administration of a country with fairness. And we have already explained in the fourth chapter that truth is the intellectual virtues and that peace is the virtues of character. And when these three are found, existence will be as perfect as is possible, without a doubt.

[25] Zechariah 8:16

PIRKI AVOT — Chapter 2 — Rambam

Chapter 2

1. Rabbi[1] Said: which is the straight path that a man should choose for himself? One which is an honor to

---

[1] **Rambam** - It is clear that the straight path is the good actions which we have elucidated in the fourth chapter (Eight Chapters 4), and they are the virtues of moderation. As through them a person acquires a fine disposition and he will have a good way with people. And he said it is "praiseworthy for the person adopting [it], And praiseworthy to him from [other] people." And afterwards, he said that he needs to be careful with a commandment that he thinks is light - like rejoicing in the holiday, and study of the Holy Tongue - as with a commandment the great weightiness of which is clear to you - like circumcision and tzitzit (fringes) and slaughtering of the Pesach sacrifice. And there the reason for this is for you do not know the reward given for the fulfillment of the respective commandments. And the elucidation of this matter is as I will say. And it is that the entire Torah has positive commandments and negative commandments. It is true that Scripture elucidated the punishment of each negative commandment except for a few of them. And one is obligated the death penalties for some of them and excision and death at the hand of the Heavens and lashes for some of them. And we know from all of the punishments of the negative commandments which of the prohibitions are great and which ones of them are below them. And they are eight levels: The first level - and it is the greatest of them - are those things for which one is obligated stoning. And the one below it are the ones that obligate burning. And the third are the ones that obligate killing (decapitation). And the fourth are the ones that obligate strangling. And the fifth are ones that obligate excision. And the sixth are ones that obligate death at the hand of the Heavens. And the seventh are ones that obligate lashes. And the eighth are negative commandments for which we do not give lashes. And from these levels we can know what is the

weightiness of a sin or its lightness. But what is the reward from God, may He be blessed, of each of the positive commandments is not elucidated. And all of this is so that we do not know which commandment requires that we keep it much and which commandment is below it. Rather He commanded to do matter x and y and He did not make known the reward of which one of them is greater from God, may He be blessed. And because of this one needs to be careful about all of them. And because of this principle, they said (Sukkah 25a), "One who is engaged in a commandment is exempt from [another] commandment," without comparing [the weight of] the commandment that he is involved in to the other one from which he is refraining. And for this, they also said (Pesachim 64b et. al.), "We do not skip over commandments," meaning to say that when you chance upon the performance of a commandment, do not skip over it and leave it to do another commandment. And afterwards he said that even though the [relative] desirability of each commandment is not elucidated, there is an angle of comparison. And that is that every positive commandment wherein you find that one who transgresses it is obligated a great punishment, know that there is also a great reward in doing [the commandment]. And the example of this is that circumcision, slaughtering the Pesach sacrifice, resting on the seventh [day] and the making of a parapet are all positive commandments. Yet the obligation of one who does work on Shabbat is stoning, but the one who refrains from circumcision or the sacrifice on the holiday is obligated [only] excision and the one who 'places blood in his house' (by refraining from setting up a parapet) violates a negative commandment [without a tangible punishment], and that is that which is stated (Deuteronomy 22:8), "do not place blood in your house." And from here you know that the reward of Shabbat is greater than the reward of circumcision and the reward of circumcision is greater with God, may He be blessed, than the reward of making a parapet. And that is the matter of his saying, "Also, weigh the loss [that may be sustained through the fulfillment] of a commandment against the reward [that may be obtained] for [fulfilling] it." And he also said "the gain of a

PIRKI AVOT — Chapter 2 — Rambam

the person adopting it, and [on account of which] honor [accrues] to him from others. And be careful with a light commandment as with a grave one, for you did know not the reward for the fulfillment of the commandments. Also, reckon the loss [that may be sustained through the fulfillment] of a commandment against the reward [accruing] thereby, and the gain [that may be obtained through the committing] of a transgression against the loss [entailed] thereby. Apply your mind to three things and you will not come into the clutches of sin: Know what there is above you: an eye that sees, an ear that hears, and all your deeds are written in a book.

2. Rabban Gamaliel the son of Rabbi Judah Hanasi said[2]: excellent is the study of the Torah when

---

transgression," when you do not do it - this too is not elucidated. However, you can learn it from the punishment of the sin. When the sin for which the sinner was punished is great, the reward for his refraining from it is according to that level of greatness, as is elucidated in Kiddushin 39b in their saying, "Anyone who sits and does not commit a sin is given a reward like the one who does a commandment" - and we have already explained it there. And the expression of the Torah of actions being known to Him, may He be blessed, is like that when our teacher Moshe, peace be upon him, stated (Exodus 32:32), "from Your book that you have written."

[2] **Rambam** - By derekh erets (the way of the world), he meant involvement in a livelihood. And his saying, "and leads to sin" is as I explained it in another place [about] their saying (Kiddushin 29a), "In the end he will steal from the creatures." And about his saying, "And as for you, I credit you with a great reward, as if you [yourselves] had done it [on your own]," it is the word of God to those who work for the community. As sometimes they are prevented from doing a commandment while they are occupied with the needs of the community. And he said

PIRKI AVOT — Chapter 2 — Rambam

combined with a worldly occupation, for toil in them both keeps sin out of one's mind; But [study of the] Torah which is not combined with a worldly occupation, in the end comes to be neglected and becomes the cause of sin. And all who labor with the community, should labor with them for the sake Heaven, for the merit of their forefathers sustains them the community, and the forefather's righteousness endures for ever; And as for you, [God in such case says] I credit you with a rich reward, as if you [yourselves] had [actually] accomplished [it all].

3. Be[3] careful [in your dealings] with the ruling authorities for they do not befriend a person except for their own needs; they seem like friends when it is to their own interest, but they do not stand by a man in the hour of his distress.

4. He used to say: do His will as though it were your will, so that He will do your will as though it were His. Set aside your will in the face of His will, so that he may set aside the will of others for the sake of your will. Hillel said[4]: do not separate yourself from the

---

that God, may He be blessed, counts the reward upon them as if they had done that commandment even though they did not do it, since they were involved with the needs of the community for the [sake of the] name of Heaven.

[3] **Rambam** - We have already explained (Rambam Pirkei Avot 1:10) that the government (rishut) is the authorities in the early days. And he is recounting their traits and warning about them.

[4] **Rambam** - We have already made known in the fourth chapter that there is no reason to separate from the community except due to their dereliction, as we explained over there. And he said that even though a person has a distinctive character trait in his soul and he has strengthened it, he should not remove his hand

PIRKI AVOT — Chapter 2 — Rambam

community. Do not trust in yourself until the day of your death. Do not judge your fellow man until you have reached his place. Do[5] not say something that cannot be understood trusting that in the end it will be understood. Say not[6]: 'when I shall have leisure I shall study; perhaps you will not have leisure.

5. He used to say[7]: A brute is not sin-fearing, nor is an ignorant person pious; nor can a timid person learn, nor can an impatient person teach; nor will someone who engages too much in business become wise. In a place where there are no men, strive to be a man.

---

from redoubling his doing good and adding to its reinforcement. And he should not be certain [about it] and say, "This virtue has already reached my hand and it is impossible that it will fall away." As it is possible that it will fall away. And that is [the meaning] of his saying, "until the day of your death."

[5] **Rambam** - And something that cannot be heard is that the simple meaning of the words be very distant and negligible. And [only] when the person examines them carefully will he see that they are true words. And he warns against this path of speech, as he says, "Do not have your words require a distant explanation and extra examination and [only] then will the listener understand them."

[6] **Rambam** - "When I will be available": He means with this, when I am available from this business (not busy). And this is similar to what preceded of the commands of his colleague, Shammai (Avot 1:15), "Make your Torah fixed."

[7] **Rambam** - He used to say: A brute is not sin-fearing, nor is an ignorant person pious; nor can a timid person learn, nor can an impatient person teach; nor will someone who engages too much in business become wise. In a place where there are no men, strive to be a man.

6. Moreover, he[8] saw a skull floating on the face of the water. He said to it: because you drowned others, they drowned you. And in the end, they that drowned you will be drowned.

7. He used to say: The more flesh, the more worms; The more property, the more anxiety; The more wives, the more witchcraft; The more female slaves, the more lewdness; The more slaves, the more robbery; [But] the more Torah, the more life; The more sitting [in the company of scholars], the more wisdom; The more counsel, the more understanding; The more charity, the more peace. If one acquires a good name, he has acquired something for himself; If one acquires for himself knowledge of Torah, he has acquired life in the world to come.

---

[8] **Rambam** - He means to say that you were killed because you killed someone else. And the one who killed you will be be killed in the future. The intent of this statement is that bad actions will return upon the head of their doers, as he stated (Proverbs 5:22), "The wicked man will be trapped in his iniquities." And he stated (Psalms 7:16), "He has dug a pit and deepened it, [etc.]." And the sages said (Sanhedrin 90a), "With the measure that a person measures, [so] is he measured." And it is something that is apparent to the eye at every moment and every time and every place that anyone who does evil and creates types of violence and vice is himself injured by those same evils that he created - since he taught the craft that would cause damage to him and to others. And so [too regarding] anyone who teaches a virtue [in] that he creates a good action from the good, a benefit of that action will reach him - since he taught a thing that will do good to him and to others. And the words about this in the verse are very good - he stated (Job 34:11), "For He pays a man his action."

PIRKI AVOT — Chapter 2 — Rambam

8. Rabban[9] Yohanan ben Zakkai received the oral tradition from Hillel and Shammai. He used to say: if you have learned much Torah, do not claim credit for yourself, because for such a purpose were you created. Rabban Yohanan ben Zakkai had five disciples and they were these: Rabbi Eliezer ben Hyrcanus, Rabbi Joshua ben Hananiah, Rabbi Yose, the priest, Rabbi Shimon ben Nethaneel and Rabbi Eleazar ben Arach. He Rabbi Johanan used to list their outstanding virtues: Rabbi Eliezer ben Hyrcanus is a plastered cistern which loses not a drop; Rabbi Joshua ben Hananiah happy is the woman that gave birth to him; Rabbi Yose, the priest, is a pious man; Rabbi Simeon ben Nethaneel is one that fears sin, And Rabbi Eleazar ben Arach is like a spring that [ever] gathers force. He [Rabbi Yohanan] used to say: if all the sages of Israel were on one scale of the balance and Rabbi Eliezer ben Hyrcanus on the other scale, he would outweigh them all. Abba Shaul said in his name: if all the sages of Israel were on one scale of the balance, and Rabbi Eliezer ben Hyrcanus

---

[9] **Rambam** - He praised Rabbi Eliezer for his good memory in comparing him to a plastered pit that does not lose its waters. And he praised Rabbi Yehoshua for the virtues of character, in that through them is a person made happy and honored and most of the world will love him. And because of this the one who gave birth to him is happy with him. And he praised Rabbi Yose [for] virtues of good character and intellectual virtues. He praised Rabbi Shimon [for] fear of sin - and that is carefulness and striving with matters of involvement in the good and guarding from evil. And he praised Rabbi Elazar ben Arakh for good understanding and that every deep matter was easy for him and that his comprehension added to the discussion.

also with them, and Rabbi Eleazar ben Arach on the other scale, he would outweigh them all.

9. He Rabban Yohanan said unto them: go forth and observe which is the right way to which a man should cleave? Rabbi Eliezer said, a good[10] eye; Rabbi Joshua

---

[10] **Rambam** - A good eye: Sufficing with what a person has and this is from the virtues of character. And a bad eye is its opposite - meaning to say, the belittling of the things [that he has] and eagerness for increase. And his saying here, "who sees the future," the matter of which is that he studies what will be in the future from what is found now, is not from the wisdoms that it should be an intellectual virtue, and that its understanding is that he study that which is hidden from that which is revealed. Rather, what he wants with it here is the analysis about the matters of a man from his affairs through which his existence will continue, that he should investigate the end of his affairs. And he brought a metaphor corresponding to this, and that is his saying, one who borrows but does not repay, that he will not lend him another thing - and that is of the traits of vice. "But the righteous one gives graciously" (Psalms 37:21) - that is the Righteous One of the world, and He is God, may He be blessed, as it is stated (Deuteronomy 32:4), "righteous and straight is He"; and (Nehemiah 9:33), "You are righteous about all that comes upon us." The explanation is that He is generous to the man that lends to his fellow and he doesn't repay, [for] the Holy One, blessed be He, pays him in exchange for his service that he bestowed kindness to another to lend him until his hand could acquire his lacking. And when the hand [of the borrower] found it and did not pay back his lender, God, may He be blessed, paid him [instead]. And the matter of "seeing his words" is to choose and to distinguish - from the matter of "The Lord did not see" (Lamentations 3:36), the intention of which is He did not choose. And he distinguished that everything was included in his words [when] he said "a bad heart." And we have already explained in the second chapter of our introduction to the commentary on this tractate (Eight Chapters 2:2) that all of the character virtues are

said, a good companion; Rabbi Yose said, a good neighbor; Rabbi Shimon said, foresight. Rabbi Elazar said, a good heart. He [Rabban Yohanan] said to them: I prefer the words of Elazar ben Arach, for in his words your words are included. He [Rabban Yohanan] said unto them: go forth and observe which is the evil way which a man should shun? Rabbi Eliezer said, an evil eye; Rabbi Joshua said, an evil companion; Rabbi Yose said, an evil neighbor; Rabbi Shimon said, one who borrows and does not repay for he that borrows from man is as one who borrows from God, blessed be He, as it is said[11], "the wicked borrow and do not repay, but the righteous deal graciously and give". Rabbi Elazar said, an evil heart. He [Rabban Yohanan] said to them:

---

only found in the appetitive section of the soul. And in it are also found all of the character vices. And we have elucidated in the fourth chapter (Eight Chapters 4) that the actions that are good are the moderate actions which come from the virtues of character. And so [too] is it known among the philosophers and physicians that the appetitive soul is in the heart and [that] its chamber and its instruments are attributed to the heart. And even though all of the capabilities are diffused from the heart and it is its beginning according to the true opinion, the appetitive capability does not spread from it to another organ, in the way that the nutritive capability - I mean to say the vegetative capability that we discussed in the first chapter (Eight Chapters 1:7) - spreads from the heart to the liver. And understand that from everything we have elucidated that what he wanted with a good heart are the good action and they are the moderate actions and they are the virtues of character. And it includes contentment and the love of the good and others of the virtues besides this. And that is what he said, "For your words are included in his."

[11] Psalms 37:21

PIRKI AVOT — Chapter 2 — Rambam

I prefer the words of Elazar ben Arach, for in his words your words are included.

10. They each said three things: Rabbi Eliezer said[12]: Let the honor of your friend be as dear to you as your own; And be not easily provoked to anger; And[13] repent

---

[12] **Rambam** - And do not be easy to anger: Do not prepare yourself to anger and irritability. And they have already gone far in disgracing anger and irritability. And the strongest of their words is their saying (Shabbat 105b), "Anyone who gets angry is as if he worships idols." And they made it adjacent to his saying (Psalms 81:10), "You shall have no foreign god, you shall not bow to an alien god" - meaning to say that the two things are one.

[13] **Rambam** - and repent one day before your death: And [since] he does not know when he will die - maybe today or maybe tomorrow - all of his days will be in repentance. But his saying, "And warm yourself by the fire of the sages," is not from their words with which he educated them, but rather is what he heard from someone else but he would [nonetheless] recount it. And because of this it was not counted among his [three] things. And the intention of this command that he is telling you is that when you associate with the sages and with men of virtues, do not be playful with them and do not be arrogant towards them, but let your association be to let them know that you will approach them at the time that they will bring you close. And do not add to come closer to them than that which they have brought you close - that you not lose their intention about you, and you reverse their love to hate and the benefit that you hoped to get from them not reach you. And he compared this to one who warms himself by the fire - as if he sits far from it, he will enjoy its heat and get benefit from its light. But if he is negligent with himself and continues to get closer to it, he will get burnt and the benefit will turn into damage. And this is the content of his saying metaphorically, "And warm yourself by the fire of the sages, but be cautious around their coals that you should not be burned." And afterwards he added to frighten about this and he said, "Do not

one day before your death. And he also said: warm yourself before the fire of the wise, but beware of being singed by their glowing coals, for their bite is the bite of a fox, and their sting is the sting of a scorpion, and their hiss is the hiss of a serpent, and all their words are like coals of fire.

11. Rabbi Joshua said: an evil eye, the evil inclination, and hatred for humankind, put[14] a person out of the world.

12. Rabbi Yose said: Let the property of your fellow be as precious unto you as your own; Make yourself fit to study Torah for it will not be yours by inheritance;

---

think that if they bite you with their tongues that you will come back and appease them with your words and they will be appeased." As truly they will not listen to the voice of a charmer like the Seraph does not listen to it, as it stated (Psalms 55:6), "Which does not hear the voice of charmers." And you should know this from the matter of Gechazi in that which he was audacious in front of his teacher, Elisha, and who fell into a disgusting disease, as is elucidated from the words of the sages about the matter of the four men who were "leprous" (metsuarim). And so [too] with Rabbi Yehoshua ben Perachiah and with all of them is the damage that came to them elucidated - and with others that 'burnt their stew.'

[14] **Rambam** - He said that exuberance for money and much desire and badness of the soul - and that is sickness of the black bile which brings a man to be disgusted with that which his eyes see and he will hate it and he will prefer the company of animals and isolation in wildernesses and in forests and he will choose an uninhabited place, and this is with them not because of asceticism but rather because of the lack of desire and their jealousy of others - these will, without a doubt, kill a man. As his body will get sick and he will die before his time.

And[15] let all your actions be for the sake of the name of heaven.

13. Rabbi Shimon said: Be careful with the reading of Shema and the prayer, And[16] when you pray, do not make your prayer something automatic, but a plea for compassion before God, for it is said[17]: "for he is gracious and compassionate, slow to anger, abounding in kindness, and renouncing punishment"; And be not wicked in your own esteem.

14. Rabbi Elazar said: Be[18] diligent in the study of the Torah; And[19] know how to answer an epicuros, and

---

[15] **Rambam** - We have already explained in the eighth chapter (Eight Chapters 8) the matter of preparation and readiness that is needed for a person to prepare himself for the virtues. And we explained in the fifth chapter (Eight Chapters 5:8) the matter of his saying. All of your actions should be for the sake of Heaven.

[16] **Rambam** - When a man thinks of himself as lacking [virtue] and low, a lacking will not seem [too] big in his eyes for him to do it. And we have already explained that the matter of "fixed" keva is that prayer be heavy upon him and he will consider it as if he were commanded a particular chore and then he can rest from it.

[17] Joel 2:13

[18] **Rambam** - The matter of diligence (shkeidah) is from the language of the verse, "as I am diligent upon my word" (Jeremiah 1:12) - meaning to say, quick and energetic. Or its meaning would be, habit and constancy, as in "to be diligent at my doors each day" (Proverbs 8:34).

[19] **Rambam** - know what to respond to one who denigrates the Torah (epikoros): He said that you need to study things which you can respond to the epikoros from the [gentiles] and disagree with them and answer them if they challenge you. And they said, (Sanhedrin 38b), "They only taught about the gentile epikoros, but with the Jewish epikoros, if you answer him, all the more so will he rebel" - meaning to say, he will denigrate [even] more.

know before whom you toil, and that your employer is faithful, for He will pay you the reward of your labor.

15. Rabbi Tarfon said[20]: the day is short, and the work is plentiful, and the laborers are indolent, and the reward is great, and the master of the house is insistent.

16. He Rabbi Tarfon used to say: It is not your duty to finish the work, but neither are you at liberty to neglect it; If you have studied much Torah, you shall be given much reward. Faithful is your employer to pay you the reward of your labor; And[21] know that the grant of reward unto the righteous is in the age to come.

And because of this, there is no need to speak with him at all, as he has no redemption and he has completely no cure at all - as it is stated (Proverbs 2:19, "All who go to her cannot return, and they will not find the paths of life." And he said, "Even though you study the opinions of the nations to know what to answer them, guard yourself that anything from these opinions come into your heart; and know that the One before whom you serve knows what is hidden in your heart." And this is his saying, "Know before Whom you labor" - wanting to say that he directs his heart to faith in God, may He be blessed.

[20] **Rambam** - This is a metaphor for the brevity of years and multitude of wisdoms and the laziness of men to seek it, in spite of the great reward for them and the multitude of notices in the Torah and its warnings to seek wisdom and study.

[21] **Rambam** - In the future to come: He meant to say in the world to come. And we have already elucidated the [concept of the] world to come in the tenth chapter of Sanhedrin, with that which is fit to mention about it.

Chapter 3

1. Akabyah ben Mahalalel said[1]: mark well three things and you will not come into the power of sin: Know from where you come, and where you are going, and before whom you are destined to give an account and reckoning. From where do you come? From a putrid drop. Where are you going? To a place of dust, of worm and of maggot. Before whom you are destined to give an account and reckoning? Before the King of the kings of kings, the Holy One, blessed be he.

2. Rabbi Hanina, the vice-high priest said: pray for the welfare of the government, for were it not for the fear it inspires, every man would swallow his neighbor alive. Rabbi Hananiah ben Teradion said: if two sit together and there are no words of Torah spoken between them, then[2] this is a session of scorners, as it is said[3]: "nor sat he in the seat of the scornful…[rather, the teaching of the Lord is his delight]"; but if two sit

---

[1] **Rambam** - This perusal brings a person to humility - in remembering from where he came. And his perusal of his end will bring him to disparage matters of the world. And his perusal of the greatness of the Commander will bring him to be quick to listen to His commandments. And when these three come into his hand, he will not sin at all.

[2] **Rambam** - His proof that any session wherein they did not speak words of Torah is called a session of scorners is from the end of the verse (the verse after the one he cites), wherein he states (Psalms 1:2), "But rather the Torah of the Lord, etc." [It is] as if he said that because his desire was in the Torah of the Lord, he [axiomatically] did not sit in the session of scorners within which there is no Torah of the Lord.

[3] Psalms 1:1

PIRKI AVOT — Chapter 3 — Rambam

together and there are words of Torah [spoken] between them, then the Shekhinah abides among them, as it is said[4]: "then they that feared the Lord spoke one with another; and the Lord hearkened and heard, and a book of remembrance was written before Him, for them that feared the Lord and that thought upon His name". Now I have no scriptural proof for the presence of the Shekhinah except among two, how[5] do we know that even one who sits and studies Torah the Holy One, blessed be He, fixes his reward? As it is said[6]: "though

---

[4] Malachi 3:16

[5] **Rambam** - From where is there proof that that even when there is only one person sitting, etc.: In the first chapter of Berakhot 6a, it states in this language, "And from where is it derived that one who sits and engages in Torah study, the Divine Presence is with him? As it is stated: 'In every place where I cause My Name to be mentioned, I will come to you and bless you' (Exodus 20:21); Since even one, was it necessary to say two? With two, their words are written in the book of remembrance; with one, his words are not written in a book of remembrance. And since even two, was it necessary to say three? Lest you say that judgment is merely peace, and the Divine Presence does not come. Instead, we understand that sitting in judgment is also Torah. And since even three, was it necessary to say ten? With ten, the Divine Presence precedes them and comes; [with] three, not until they sit." And the explanation of "he is silent (vayidom)" as being from the hidden speech is from "a still (demamah) small voice" (I Kings 19:12). And from this did the Onkelos' Aramaic translation explain, "And Aharon was silent" (Leviticus 10:3) as "And Ahaon praised." And his proof that he is like one that observed the entire Torah completely is from his saying, "since he takes it on himself" (Lamentations 3:28) - it is as if the giving of the entire Torah was only for his sake.

[6] Lamentations 3:28

he sits alone and [meditate] in stillness, yet he takes [a reward] unto himself".

3. Rabbi Shimon said: if three have eaten at one table and have not spoken there words of Torah, it[7] is as if they had eaten sacrifices offered to the dead, as it is said[8], "for all tables are full of filthy vomit, when the All-Present is absent". But, if three have eaten at one table, and have spoken there words of Torah, [it is] as if they had eaten at the table of the All-Present, blessed be He, as it is said[9], "And He said unto me, this is the table before the Lord".

4. Rabbi Hananiah ben Hakinai said: one who wakes up at night, or walks on the way alone and turns his heart to idle matters, behold, this man is mortally guilty.

5. Rabbi Nehunia ben Hakkanah said: whoever takes upon himself the yoke[10] of the Torah, they remove from

---

[7] **Rambam** - Idolatrous sacrifices are called the offerings of the dead, as the verse (Psalms 106:28) called it, as we explained in the third chapter of Idol Worship (Rambam Mishnah Avodah Zarah 3:8). And Yishayahu also called it "vomit and feces" to disgrace it, just like idolatry itself is called dung and abominations. And before this verse is a verse that indicates occupation with food and drink and ignoring Torah and its study, and because of this the tables are all as if they ate upon them dirty things and feces - meaning to say, idolatry. And that verse is his saying before this verse, "But these are also muddled by wine and misled by ale" (Isaiah 28:7).

[8] Isaiah 28:8

[9] Ezekiel 41:22

[10] **Rambam** - The yoke of Torah: Constancy of reading it.

him the[11] yoke of government and the yoke[12] of worldly concerns, and whoever breaks off from himself the yoke of the Torah, they place upon him the yoke of government and the yoke of worldly concerns.

6. Rabbi Halafta of Kefar Hanania said: when ten sits together and occupy themselves with Torah, the Shechinah abides among them, as it is said[13]: "God stands in[14] the congregation of God". How do we know that the same is true even of five? As it is said[15]: "This band of His He has established on earth". How do we know that the same is true even of three? As it is said[16]: "In the midst of the judges He judges", How do we

---

[11] **Rambam** - The yoke of government: The exertion imposed by the king and his troops.

[12] **Rambam** - And the yoke of the way of the world (derekh erets): The exertion imposed by time. He said that as a reward for his taking the yoke of Torah, God, may He be blessed, will save him and lighten the exertion of time from upon him. And his saying, "casts from himself the yoke of Torah," is that he said, "The Torah is not from Heaven and I will not bear it." And they said (Eruvin 54a), "'Engraved (charut) on the tablets' (Exodus 32:16) freedom (cheirut) on the tablets" - meaning to say, freedom from the events of time and the matters of kings comes to the one who accepts and does what is written upon the tablets.

[13] Psalm 82:1

[14] **Rambam** - "In the congregation of God": Behold, we have explained in the beginning of Sanhedrin (Rambam on Mishnah Sanhedrin 1:6), that a congregation does not apply to less than ten. And there we also explained that a court is no less than three and they are called elohim (powers) with regard to judgement. And the explanation of "band" (bundle) is that which a man bands together in his one hand. And the hand has five fingers in it. And the group of five fingers is also called a band.

[15] Amos 9:6

[16] Psalm 82:1

know that the same is true even of two? As it is said[17]: "Then they that fear the Lord spoke one with another, and the Lord hearkened, and heard". How do we know that the same is true even of one? As it is said[18]: "In every place where I cause my name to be mentioned I will come unto you and bless you".

7. Rabbi Elazar of Bartotha said: give to Him of that which is His, for you and that which is yours is His; and thus it says with regards to David[19]: "for everything comes from You, and from Your own hand have we given you". Rabbi Jacob said: if one is studying while walking on the road and interrupts his study and says, "how fine is this tree!" [or] "how fine is this newly ploughed field!" scripture accounts it to him as if he was mortally guilty.

8. Rabbi Dostai ben Rabbi Yannai said in the name of Rabbi Meir: whoever forgets one word of his study, scripture accounts it to him as if he were mortally guilty, as it is said[20], "But take utmost care and watch yourselves scrupulously, so that you do not forget the things that you saw with your own eyes". One could have inferred that this is the case even when his study proved too hard for him, therefore scripture says[21], "that they do not fade from your mind as long as you live". Thus, he is not mortally guilty unless he deliberately removes them from his heart.

---

[17] Malachi 3:16
[18] Exodus 20:21
[19] Chronicles-1 29:14
[20] Deuteronomy 4:9
[21] Deuteronomy 4:9

PIRKI AVOT — Chapter 3 — Rambam

9. Rabbi Hanina ben Dosa said: anyone whose fear of sin precedes his wisdom, his wisdom is enduring, but anyone whose wisdom precedes his fear of sin, his wisdom is not enduring. He also used to say[22]: anyone whose deeds exceed his wisdom, his wisdom is enduring, but anyone whose wisdom exceeds his deeds, his wisdom is not enduring.

10. He used to say: one with whom men are pleased, God is pleased. But anyone from whom men are displeased, God is displeased. Rabbi Dosa ben Harkinas said[23]: morning sleep, midday wine, children's talk and sitting in the assemblies of the ignorant put a man out of the world.

11. Rabbi Elazar of Modiin said: one who profanes sacred things, and one who despises the festivals, and[24] one who causes his fellow's face to blush in public, and[25] one who annuls the covenant of our father

---

[22] **Rambam** - Behold this thing is agreed upon by the philosophers as well: That habituation of the virtues - when it comes before acquisition of wisdom to the point that it is a strong possession, and he studies wisdom afterwards such that it will give him alacrity for those goods - will add joy and love to his wisdom and industriousness to increase upon it; since [wisdom] stimulates him to do that to which he is already accustomed. But when the acquisition of knowledge comes first, and he studies the virtues afterwards, his wisdom will prevent him from that which he desires according to his habit. And so, wisdom will weigh upon him and he will leave it.

[23] **Rambam** - He said that these things prevent and remove the virtue of of a man until he leaves the world and is lost.

[24] **Rambam** - One who whitens the face of another: That is one who embarrasses his fellow.

[25] **Rambam** - nullifies the covenant: This is as its simple understanding. And there it said about all of the things that the

Abraham, may he rest in peace, and he who is contemptuous towards the Torah, even[26] though he has to his credit knowledge of the Torah and good deeds, he has not a share in the world to come.

12. Rabbi Ishmael said[27]: be suppliant to a superior, submissive under compulsory service, and[28] receive every man happily.

---

sages said that the one who does them has no share in the world to come, "About what are we speaking? If when he repented, there is nothing that stands in front of repentance. Rather it is when he did not repent but he died with afflictions." It means to say that the weight of the sins - and these are the ones about which they said he has no share in the world to come - is greater than other sins, as for the former exclusively, afflictions with death do not atone.

[26] **Rambam** - One who reveals meanings (literally, faces) in the Torah: is one transgresses the laws of the Torah in public and that is the epitome of heresy, as God, may He be blessed, said (Numbers 15:30), "And the soul that does with a high hand (publicly)." And the matter of revealing faces is that he reveals his face and is brazen - and that is an expression of heresy. And so is it explained in the gemara (Talmud Yerushalmi Peah 1:1). They said one who reveals faces in the Torah is one that transgresses the words of the Torah in public, like Yohayakim the son of Yoshayahu.

[27] **Rambam** - Be yielding (literally, light) to an elder: The meaning of lightness is known

[28] **Rambam** - And pleasant: This is calmness and ease. And he said with this command that when you are in front of a man of great standing, make yourself light towards him and serve him and stand in his presence if he wants and do not seek honor for yourself from him. But when you are with black hair - meaning to say one of young years - do not do this; but seek honor for yourself from him and do not be playful and do not be jocular with him. Afterwards he said, "You should not think that that which I have warned you from being jocular with someone of

13. Rabbi Akiva said: Merriment and frivolity accustom one to sexual licentiousness; Tradition is a fence to the Torah; Tithes a fence to wealth, Vows[29] a fence to abstinence; A fence to wisdom is silence.

14. He used to say[30]: Beloved is man for he was created in the image [of God]. Especially beloved is he for it was made known to him that he had been created in the image of God, as it is said[31]: "for in the image of God

---

young years obligates that you should greet him with rage and with a choleric face. This is not the intention. Rather you need to greet every person - small or big, freeman or slave, every man of the human species - with joy." And this is more than that which Shammai said (Avot 1:15), "with a pleasant countenance." The translator said it appears to me from the words of the teacher (Rambam) that he explains the word mekabel (literally, receive) from hakbelat panim (being across from the face) which is as if he is across. This is derived from (Exodus 26:5) "the loops across (makbilot)," which he translated from the Aramaic as across or facing. And also, in Arabic one says about this matter an expression of meeting and being opposite - one says x met me happily or angrily. And with this type of expression did the teacher explain mekabel here - and know it.

[29] **Rambam** - When a man makes vows and keeps them, the acquisition of keeping away from that which he wants to keep away from comes into his hand, and that acquisition is strengthened for him. And abstinence becomes easier for him, meaning to say guarding from impurities - as they said in Chagigah (Mishnah Chagigah 2:7), "The clothes of an am ha'arets unlearned person are midras (considered impure by treading) for the abstinent.

[30] **Rambam** - He would say that revelation of that which He benefited him a certain good is a separate benefit. As there are times when a man benefits another man by way of mercy and does not reveal the certain thing that he did for him because he is too lowly in his eyes.

[31] Genesis 9:6

He made man". Beloved are Israel in that they were called children to the All-Present. Especially beloved are they for it was made known to them that they are called children of the All-Present, as it is said[32]: "your are children to the Lord your God". Beloved are Israel in that a precious vessel was given to them. Especially beloved are they for it was made known to them that the desirable instrument, with which the world had been created, was given to them, as it is said[33]: "for I give you good instruction; forsake not my teaching".

15. Everything[34] is foreseen yet freedom of choice is granted, And the world is judged with goodness; And

---

[32] Deuteronomy 14:1

[33] Proverbs 4:2

[34] **Rambam** - This statement includes great things and [so] it is fitting that this statement would be of Rabbi Akiva. And this is its explanation in brief on condition that you know all that came before it in the earlier chapters. He said [that] all that is in the world is known to Him, may He be blessed and He comprehends it. And that is his saying, "Everything is foreseen." And afterwards he said [that] you should not think that in His knowing actions [in the future], it is obligated by necessity - meaning to say that a person is forced in his actions to [do one] action out of the [many] actions. The matter is not like this, but [rather] freewill is in the hand of a man as to what he will do. And this is his saying, "and freewill is given." He means to say that freewill is given to every man, as we elucidated in the eighth chapter (Eight Chapters 8). And he said that the judgement of God, may He be blessed, with people, however, is with kindness and good - not according to the judgement that befits them, as He, may He be blessed, explained (Numbers 18:30), "of great patience and much kindness and truth" - and the rabbis, may their memory be blessed, said "'of great patience' with the righteous and the evil." And the prophet (recounter) said (Psalms 145:9), "Good to all is the Lord." And afterwards he said that the virtues

everything is in accordance with the preponderance of works.

16. He used to say: everything is given against a pledge, and a net is spread out over all the living; the store is open, and[35] the storekeeper allows credit, but the ledger

---

do not come to a man according to the quantity of the greatness of the deed, but rather according to the great number of good deeds. And this is that indeed the virtues arrive by repetition of the good deeds many times. And with this does a strong acquisition come - not when a man does one great deed from the good deeds; as from this alone, a strong acquisition will not come to him. And the parable with this is that when a man gives a thousand gold coins at one time to one man to whom it is fitting and he does not give anything to another man; the trait of generosity will not come into his hand with this great act, as [much as] it will come to one who donates a thousand gold pieces a thousand times and gives each one of them out of generosity. [This is] because this one repeated the act of generosity a thousand times and a strong acquisition of it came to him [in this way]. But [the other] only aroused his soul with a great arousal towards a good act, and afterwards it ceased from him. And so [too] with Torah, the reward of the one who redeems one captive with a hundred dinar or [gives] charity to a poor person with a hundred dinar which is enough for what he lacks is not like the one who redeems ten captives or fills the lack of ten poor people - each one with ten dinar. And in this comparison and this matter is that which he said, " in accordance to the majority of the deed" - and not in accordance to the greatness of the deed.

[35] **Rambam** - The shopkeeper grants credit: One who gives much time with a debt and does not request it immediately. And this parable is clear and its intention is known. And that which he said, "and everyone who wants to borrow can come and borrow," strengthens the earlier matter that there is no necessity [forcing actions], but with free choice does a man do what he wants to do. And his saying, "and the collectors go constantly"

is open and the hand writes, and whoever wishes to borrow may come and borrow; but the collectors go round regularly every day and exact dues from man, either with his consent or without his consent, and they have that on which they can rely in their claims, seeing that the judgment is a righteous judgment, and[36] everything is prepared for the banquet.

17. Rabbi Elazar ben Azariah said[37]: Where there is no Torah, there is no right conduct; where there is no right

---

is a metaphor for death and other punishments that come to a man.

[36] **Rambam** - and everything is prepared for the feast: This is to say the ultimate intention of all this is life in the world to come.

[37] **Rambam** - He means to say with this that each of these two - each one of the two of them - helps the existence of the other and completes the other one. However, his words about knowledge (daat) and understanding (binah) is a very subtle matter with the philosophers; and I will mention it [and] rely upon the understanding of the one that will investigate it. And that is that the knowledge that reaches us and that we acquire is, indeed, the comprehension of ideas that we comprehend if we separate the form and comprehend it or if we comprehend the separated forms in their [pristine] existence - without our making them knowledge, for they, themselves, are knowledge. And that comprehension is called understanding, and that is [the acquisition] of knowledge. And with knowledge, too, we understand [it] and it becomes possible to comprehend what we comprehend. And it is as if he said that if we do not comprehend an idea, we do not have knowledge; and if we do not have knowledge, we can not comprehend an idea - as we comprehend it with knowledge. And understanding this thing is very difficult - even from the books that are written about it, all the more so here. However, we are only straightening out the straight path to it. Any one whose deeds: We have already explained and elucidated these things in this chapter in the words of Rabbi Chaninah ben Dosa (Rambam Pirkei Avot 3:9).

conduct, there is no Torah. Where there is no wisdom there is no fear of God; where there is no fear of God, there is no wisdom. Where there is no understanding, there is no knowledge; where there is no knowledge, there is no understanding. Where there is no bread, there is no Torah; where there is no, Torah there is no bread. He used to say: one whose wisdom exceeds his deeds, to what may he be compared? To a tree whose branches are numerous but whose roots are few, so that when the wind comes, it uproots it and overturns it, as it is said[38], "He shall be like a bush in the desert, which does not sense the coming of good. It is set in the scorched places of the wilderness, in a barren land without inhabitant". But one whose deeds exceed his wisdom, to what may he be compared? To a tree whose branches are few but roots are many, so that even if all the winds in the world come and blow upon it, they cannot move it out of its place, as it is said[39], "He shall be like a tree planted by waters, sending forth its roots by a stream. It does not sense the coming of heat, its leaves are ever fresh. It has no care in a year of drought; it does not cease to yield fruit".

18. Rabbi Eliezer Hisma said: the laws of mixed bird offerings and the key to the calculations of menstruation days these, these are the body of the halakhah. The calculation of the equinoxes and gematria are the desserts of wisdom.

---

[38] Jeremiah 17:6
[39] Jeremiah 17:8

Chapter 4

1. Ben Zoma said[1]: Who is wise? He who learns from every man, as it is said[2]: "From all who taught me have I gained understanding". Who is mighty? He who subdues his evil inclination, as it is said[3]: "He that is slow to anger is better than the mighty; and he that rules his spirit than he that takes a city". Who is rich? He who rejoices in his lot, as it is said[4]: "You shall enjoy the fruit of your labors, you shall be happy and you shall prosper", "You shall be happy" in this world, "and you shall prosper" in the world to come. Who is he that is honored? He who honors his fellow human beings as it is said[5]: "For I honor those that honor Me, but those who spurn Me shall be dishonored".

2. Ben Azzai said[6]: Be quick in performing a minor commandment as in the case of a major one, and flee

---

[1] **Rambam** - This is clear and we have already elucidated its matter in the previous chapters.
[2] Psalms 119:99
[3] Proverbs 16:3
[4] Psalms 128:2
[5] I Samuel 2:30
[6] **Rambam** - We have already elucidated the explanation of this statement in Chapter 10 of Sanhedrin. And the sages, peace be upon them, have already brought attention to a wonderful innovation in the Torah in which there is inducement to the performance of the commandments. And it is its stating (Deuteronomy 4:41), "Then Moshe separated three cities in Transjordan, etc.," while knowing that they would not be effective - as they would not have the [status] of cities of refuge until the three others in the Land of Israel would be separated. They said (Makkot 10a), "Our teacher Moshe, peace be upon

from transgression; For one commandment leads to another commandment, and transgression leads to another transgression; For the reward for performing a commandment is another commandment and the reward for committing a transgression is a transgression.

3. He used to say[7]: do not despise any man, and do not discriminate against anything, for there is no man that has not his hour, and there is no thing that has not its place.

4. Rabbi Levitas a man of Yavneh said[8]: be exceeding humble spirit, for the end of man is the worm. Rabbi

---

him, knew that these three cities in Transjordan do not shelter until the three cities in the Land of Israel would be separated, as it is stated (Numbers 35:13), 'they shall be six cities of refuge.' And he separated these nonetheless, since he said, 'Since a commandment has come to my hand, I will perform it.'" And if our teacher Moshe, peace be upon him - the fathomer of the truths, the [most] complete of the complete - was eager to add half of a positive commandment upon all of his rank and wholeness in this way, there is no need to say that those whose souls are leprous and their leprosy is strong and gaining should do so.

[7] **Rambam** - And he said it is impossible that there not be for every man a time in which he can damage or benefit, and even with a small thing.

[8] **Rambam** - We have already elucidated and mentioned in the earlier chapters that humility is from the highest of traits. And it is the mean between pride and lowliness of spirit and it has no other name - just humility. But there are many names for pride: In the Hebrew language, high heart, elevated eyes, proud and high. And from the names of the sages, may their memory be blessed, [are] a high spirit, coarse-spirited and uppity. And across from them is lowliness of spirit. We have already explained in the fourth chapter (Eight Chapters 4:7) that a person

PIRKI AVOT — Chapter 4 — Rambam

needs to incline a little to one of the extremes until he establishes himself in the middle of, as a [type of] fence. But only in this trait from [all] the other traits - meaning to say with pride - due to the great deficiency of this trait for the pious ones and their knowledge of its damage, they distanced themselves to the other extreme and completely inclined towards lowliness of spirit, until there was no room for pride in their souls at all. And behold, I saw in a book from the books on characteristics that one of the important pious men was asked and told, "Which day is the one upon which you rejoiced more than any of your days?" He said [back], "The day that I was going on a boat and my place was in the lowest places of the boat among the packages of clothing, and there were traders and men of means on the boat as well. And I was laying in my place and one of the men of the boat got up to urinate and I was insignificant in his eyes and lowly - as I was very low in his eyes - to the point that he revealed his nakedness and urinated on me. And I was astonished by the intensification of the trait of brazenness in his soul. But, as God lives, my soul was not pained by his act at all and my strength was not aroused. And I rejoiced with a great joy that I reached the extreme that the disgrace of this empty one did not pain me and [that] my soul did not feel [anything] towards him." And it is without a doubt that this is the extreme of low spiritedness, to the point of being distanced from pride. And I will now mention a little of what the sages mentioned in praise of humility and [in] disgrace of pride. And it is because of this that this one commanded to come close to lowliness and said, "Be very, very lowly in spirit" - out of his fear that a person remain only in humility, all the more so that there be a trace of pride in him. As it is close to it, since modesty is the mean, as we mentioned. And they said (Talmud Yerushalmi Shabbat 1:3) in praise of humility [that like] that which wisdom made a crown for its head, humility made a sole for its heel - the explanation of which is its shoe - as it is written (Psalms 111:10), "The beginning of wisdom is the fear of God." This is a proof that fear of God is greater than wisdom, as it is a cause for its existence. And it states (Proverbs 22:4), "[At the] heel of humility is the fear of sin," which is to say that you will find the fear of God at the heels of humility. If so, humility is much greater than wisdom. And they said (Megillah 31a), "This thing is written in the Torah and repeated in the Prophets and tripled in the Writings; every place that you find the greatness of the Holy One, blessed be He, you find His modesty: It is written in the Torah (Deuteronomy 10:17), 'the great God, etc.' And it is written after it (Deuteronomy 10:18), 'Who does the judgment of the orphan and the widow.' And it is repeated in the Prophets, as it is written (Isaiah 57:15), 'So speaks He who high aloft forever dwells, whose name is holy, "I dwell on high, in holiness."' And adjacent to it is '"with the contrite and the lowly in spirit."' And it is tripled in the Writings, as it is written (Psalms 68:5), 'extol Him who rides the clouds; the Lord is His name.' And it is written after it (Psalms 68:6), 'the Father of orphans and the Judge of widows.'" And you should learn from our teacher, Moshe, peace be upon him, in whom the intellectual virtues and the dispositional virtues were perfected - all of them directed to the level of prophecy - the master of Torah, the master of wisdom. And [yet] God, may He be blessed, praised him over every man with the trait of humility and stated (Numbers 12:3), "and Moshe the man is very humble, more than any person." And His stating, "very" is a sign of his great modesty and his inclining towards the side of the far extreme. And so, you will find him state (Exodus 16:7) "and what are we?" And so too with David, 'the anointed of the God of Yaakov, the pleasant singer of the praises of Israel.' And he was an honored king, whose kingdom grew great and sword grew strong and who God, may He be blessed, designated through our teacher Moshe, peace be upon him, since he is the star that proceeded from Yaakov (Numbers 24:17), as the sages, may their memory be blessed, elucidated. And he was a prophet and the greatest of of the seventy elders [of his time], as he stated (II Samuel 23:8), "who sat in the sitting of the wise." And with all of this, he stated [about himself] (Psalms 51:19), "and a heart broken and crushed, God will not disgrace." And he increased in these virtues that indicate extreme modesty. And [the following is from] what the rabbis, may their memory be blessed, said about pride. They said (Sotah 4b), "Any man that has coarse-spiritedness is like he worshiped idolatry. Here it is written (Proverbs 16:5), 'An abomination of the Lord is anyone of a high heart'; and there it is written (Deuteronomy 7:26), 'And do not bring an abomination into your house.'" And they said, "It is like he denied a fundamental [of faith], as it is stated (Deuteronomy 8:14), 'And your heart grow high and you forget the Lord.'" And they said that the sin of pride is like one who has forbidden sexual relations: It states [about the latter] (Leviticus 18:27), "As they did all of these abominations." And they said (Sotah 4b) that one who becomes uppity is he, himself - for God - like idolatry itself. And they brought a proof from the statement (Isaiah 2:22), "'Cease from man, whose soul is in his nose' - meaning to say, of a high (haughty) spirit - 'for by what (vameh) is he estimated?' - do not read it as vameh, but rather bamah (an altar, as both words are written with the same three letters)." And they said [about] one that becomes uppity that it is fitting to kill him. And they said (Sotah 5a) that anyone who has coarse spirit in him is fitting to be cut down like a tree-god. It is written here (Isaiah 10:33), "the ones of high stature cut down"; and there it is written (Deuteronomy 7:5), "and their tree-gods shall you cut down." And they said that God, may He be blessed, will not revive during the revival of the dead those that became uppity. [This was] their saying, "Any man that has coarse spirit in him, his dust will not be aroused; as it is stated (Isaiah 27:19), 'awake and shout for joy, you who dwell in the dust': he who was made dust in his life - meaning to say the humble ones - they are the ones that will be revived." And they emphasized this and said that any man that has coarse spirit in him, the Divine Presence cries out about him; as it is stated (Psalms 138:6), "and the high ones from afar, He makes known." And they elaborated with their words. They said in saying that tsaarat (a Biblical form of leprosy) is a punishment for the haughty ones, "For a swelling (seiat), for a rash, or for a discoloration" (Leviticus 14:56) - and a swelling is only height (haughtiness), as it is stated (Isaiah 2:14), "the elevated (nisaot) hills." It is as if it said to the one who becomes uppity is a swelling [of tsaarat]. And the end is what they said

PIRKI AVOT — Chapter 4 — Rambam

Yohanan ben Berokah said[9]: whoever profanes the name of heaven in secret, he shall be punished in the

---

(Sotah 5a), 'In excommunication is the one that has it and in excommunication is the one that does not have it at all.'" [This] means to say that a person should not be humble in spirit to the final extreme, as it is not from the virtues. And they quantified it metaphorically - one in sixty-four parts, meaning to say if we place pride in one corner and lowliness of spirit in another corner, there would be sixty-four parts along the spectrum. And he should stand in the sixty-third section. He does not only want the mean with this trait, so as to escape from pride. As if he were to be missing [just] one section and [proportionately] come closer to pride, he would be put in excommunication. And that is the opinion of Rava about humility. But Rav Nachman decided and said that it is not fitting for a man to have from it - meaning to say from pride - not a large a section and not a small section, as its sin is not small. That which makes man into an abomination is not fitting to [even] approach. They said about this matter, "Rav Nachman bar Yitschak said, 'Not form it and not from part of it. And is it a small thing that which is written, 'An abomination of the Lord is anyone of a high heart?'" And to strengthen [precaution] from this cursed sin, Rabbi Levitas said, "Be very, very lowly in spirit for the hope of man is worms" - meaning to say that you need to force yourself until you have distanced yourself from pride, by your thinking of the end of the body, and that is its return to worms.

[9] **Rambam** - You know from Scripture that the unintentional transgressor has a sin. And because of this, he needs atonement with a sacrifice. And God, may He be blessed, said about him, "And he is forgiven from his sin that he sinned." But he is not like the intentional sinner. God forbid, for the One of the straight paths, God - may He be blessed - to equate the intentional with the unintentional in [any] thing from the things. Rather his intention here is that the desecration of the Name, whether it is intentional or unintentional, will be punished publicly - if it was intentional, the punishment for intentional, if it was

open. Unwittingly or wittingly, it is all one in profaning the name.

5. Rabbi Ishmael his son said: He who learns in order to teach, it is granted to him to study and to teach; But he who learns in order to practice, it is granted to him to learn and to teach and to practice. Rabbi Zadok said[10]:

---

unintentional, the punishment for unintentional. But both punishments are public.

[10] **Rambam** - After I decided not to speak about this testament because it is clear and since, according to my opinion, my words will not please most of the great Torah sages - and perhaps any of them - I went back on my decision and I will speak about it, without paying attention to the earlier or contemporary rabbis. Know that that which he said not to make the Torah into a spade with which to dig - meaning to say, do not consider it a tool to live by - he explained and said that anyone who benefits in this world from the honor of Torah removes his life from the world - the explanation of which is, from life in the world to come. Yet people have missed this obvious language and thrown it over the backs. And they have depended upon understandings of the words that they [themselves] did not understand - and I will explain them. And they established rules for themselves upon individuals and upon communities, and they brought people to think in their total foolishness that it is mandatory and fitting that they help the sages and their students and the people involved in Torah, and for whom their Torah [study] is their craft. And this is all a mistake, and nothing is found in the Torah or in the words of the rabbis, may their memory be blessed, that substantiates it or gives it a basis to rest upon at all. As when we look into the words of the rabbis, may their memory be blessed, we do not find among them that they were requesting money from people and they did not collect money for the honored and precious academies, nor for the heads of the exiles, nor for their judges, nor for the promulgators of Torah - not for one of their greats and not for any people of the nation. Rather, we find in each and every generation in all of their communities that there were

PIRKI AVOT   Chapter 4   Rambam

among [the Torah scholars] poor men of extreme poverty and wealthy men of extreme wealth. And God forbid that I should suspect those generations of not being doers of kindness and givers of charity. As if such a poor man had extended his hand to receive it, they would have filled his house with gold and pearls; but he did not want [it]. Rather he sufficed with [the earnings from] the work in which he engaged - whether comfortably or with duress - and he was loath of what [came from] the hand of people, since the Torah prevented him from it. And you already know that Hillel the Elder was a wood chopper and that he studied in front of Shemaya and Avtalyon and he was extremely poor. And his rank was such that you know that some of his students were compared to Moshe, Aharon and Yehoshua; and the least of his students was Rabban Yochanan ben Zakkai. And there is no doubt to the intelligent one that if he had instructed the people of his generation to let him benefit from them, they would not have allowed him to be a wood chopper. And also Rabbi Chaninah ben Dosa - about whom a heavenly voice went out and said, "The whole world is only nourished for the sake of my son, Chaninah; and my son, Chaninah, has enough with a kav of carobs from one Shabbat eve to [the next] Shabbat eve" (Berakhot 17b) - yet he did not request [anything] from people. And Karna was a judge in the Land of Israel and he was a water drawer. And when litigants would come in front of him, he would say, "Give me someone to draw [the water] in my place or [the wage from] my absence and I will adjudicate for you." And the Jews in that generation were not not cruel and were not lacking in doing kindness. And we do not find any sage of the poor sages that reviled the people of his generation for not making them rich - God forbid for them [to have done so]. Rather they believed in God, may He be blessed, and in the Torah of Moshe, through which a person merits life in the world to come. And [so] they did not allow themselves to request money from people. And they saw that taking it was a desecration of [God's] name in the eyes of the masses, because they would think that Torah is a profession from the professions though which a person lives and it will become disgraced in their eyes. And [so] the one that would do this, 'the word of God, he will disgrace.' However the ones that drew strength to disagree with the truth and with simple and obvious verses by taking people's money - whether voluntarily or against their will - were misled by stories that are found in the Gemara about people that [were disabled] or elderly, having come up in days, such that it was impossible for them to do work. As there was no strategy for them [to survive] except for the taking of money from others. And if not, what would they do - should they die? And the Torah did not command this. And you will find that the story that they bring as a proof (Bava Metzia 84b) when they said 'she was like merchant ships, from far does she bring her bread,' is about [someone disabled] who was not able to do work. But with the ability [to do work], the Torah does not create [such] a path. And Rabbi Yosef would carry wood from place to place and would say, "(Beautiful) [Great] is work, as it heats up its master" - meaning to say with the effort of his limbs. Since by carrying the heavy wood, he would heat up his body without a doubt. And he would praise this and be happy with it. And he derived pleasure from that which God, may He be blessed, apportioned to him, that which was for him from the virtues of sufficing. And I have heard the crazy and confused ones base themselves on the proof that they bring from their saying (Berakhot 10b), "One who seeks to benefit, let him benefit like Elisha; and one who does not seek to benefit, let him not benefit like Shmuel from Rama." And this is not at all similar to what they are bringing. Rather, for me, it is a great mistake to bring a proof from it, as it is clear and there is no room for a person to make a mistake in it. As Elisha did not take money from people - all the more so did he not request [it] from them and establish rules for them, God forbid. Instead, he would only take honor when someone gave him lodging when he passed by, to be in his home. And he would eat his bread on that night or on that day and he would return to his affairs. But Shmuel would not enter the home of a person and would not eat from any man. And about something like this the sages, may their memory be blessed, said that if a Torah scholar wants to emulate this to the point that he not enters the house of any person, that right is in his hand. But if he wants to lodge with people in his passing by them for the needs of his travel expenses, that right is [also] in his hand. As they already warned about eating [as a guest of] any man when it is not necessary. And they said (Pesachim 49a), "A Torah scholar that proliferates his meal in every place, etc." And they [also] said, "It is forbidden for a Torah scholar to benefit from any meal that is not [pertinent] to a commandment." And why should I write at length about this matter. Instead, I will mention a story which elucidates it in the Gemara (Nedarim 62a). And it is that a [certain] man had a vineyard in which thieves would enter. And each time he would see them on each day he [would] find his fruit lessening progressively. And he did not have a doubt that one of the thieves put his eye upon it. And [so], he was pained by this all the days of the harvest until he harvested what [was left for him to] harvest. And he put them out to dry until they dried and he gathered in the raisins. And the way of people when they gather dried fruit is that a few individual figs or grapes would fall. And it is permissible to eat them because they are ownerless and the owners already left them for their finders due to their small quantity. And Rabbi Tarfon came one day to that vineyard by chance and he sat and took from the raisins that fell and ate them. And the owner of the field thought that this was the thief that stole from him the whole year - and he did not recognize [Rabbi Tarfon] but had heard of him. And [so] he immediately took him and overpowered him and placed him in a sack and placed him on his back to throw him into the river. And when Rabbi Tarfon saw this, he yelled out and said, "Woe to Tarfon, for this man is killing him." And when the owner of the vineyard heard, he left him and ran away, knowing that he had sinned a great sin. But Rabbi Tarfon was distressed from that day onwards all of his days and he mourned about that which happened to him, as he saved himself through the honor of the Torah, while he was very rich and could have said, "Leave me and I will give you such and such gold coins." And he could have given them to him and he did not need to inform him that that he was Rabbi Tarfon. And [that way] he would have saved himself

PIRKI AVOT — Chapter 4 — Rambam

with his money and not with Torah. And they said, "All the days of that righteous man, he was distressed over this matter, saying, 'Woe is me, for I made use of the crown of Torah'" - as anyone who use the crown of Torah does not have a share in the world to come and is uprooted from the world. And they said about this, "It was since Rabbi Tarfon was very rich, and he should have appeased him with money." And so [too, the story that] Rebbi (Rabbi Yehuda Hanassi) opened his storehouses in a year of drought and said, "Anyone who wants to come and take his sustenance, let him come and sustain himself, but only if he is a Torah scholar." And Rabbi Yochanan ben Amram came and stood in front of him and he did not recognize him; he said, "Rebbi, sustain me." He said [back] to him, "Have you read scripture?" "No." "Have you studied mishnah?" "No." "[If so], with (in the merit of) what should I sustain you?" He said, "Sustain me like a dog or a raven" - meaning to say, even though there is no wisdom in me, just like God, may He be blessed, sustains the impure animal and the impure bird - as an ignoramus is no less than them. And he gave him. But afterwards he regretted [it], since he had seduced him with his words and he said, "Woe to me, since I benefited an ignoramus from my possessions." And the listeners of what happened to him said to him, "Maybe it was Yonatan ben Amram, your student, who does not want to benefit through the honor of Torah, when he could avoid it - and even with a ruse." And he investigated and found that it was so. And these two stories will silence anyone who disagrees about this matter. The things that the Torah did, however, permit to the Torah scholar are that they should give their money to a man to do business according to his choice and the profit will be all for them, if he wants. And one who does this has a great reward for it - and this is "the one who puts merchandise into the 'pocket' of a Torah scholar." And [also] that their merchandise be sold before all [other] merchandise, and that [things] be purchased for them at the beginning of the market [session]. These are rules that God, may He be blessed, established, [just] like He established the gifts for the priest and the tithes for the Levite - according to that which has been

do not make them a crown for self-exaltation, nor a spade with which to dig. So too Hillel used to say, "And he that puts the crown to his own use shall perish." Thus, you have learned, anyone who derives worldly benefit from the words of the Torah, removes his life from the world.

6. Rabbi Yose said: whoever honors[11] the Torah is himself honored by others, and whoever dishonors the Torah is himself dishonored by others.

7. Rabbi Ishmael his son said: he who refrains himself from judgment, rids himself of enmity, robbery and

---

received by tradition. As these two actions are done by some businessmen towards each other by way of honor and even though there is no wisdom [to be honored] - a Torah scholar is worthwhile to be like an honored ignoramus. And the Torah eased the rules upon Torah scholars [regarding] taxes and quartering troops and [taxes] specific to each person, and that is called the poll tax - the community pays it for them. And so too with revenue for the building of walls and similar to them. And even if a Torah scholar is endowed with money, he is not obligated in anything of all this. And Rabbi Yosef Halevi, may his memory be blessed, already instructed a man in a certain place who had gardens and orchards and was obligated to pay thousands of gold coins in taxes on their account - and he said that he would be exempted from giving anything on their account from all that we have mentioned, since he was a Torah scholar. And [this is so] although even a poor man in Israel would give this tax. And this is a law of the Torah, just like the Torah exempted the priests from the half shekel that even the poor had to pay - as we have elucidated in its place - and that which is similar to it.

[11] **Rambam** - Honor of the Torah is in teaching alacrity in its performance and honoring the sages that support it and the books that they wrote about it. And so too, desecration of the Torah is the opposite of these three.

false swearing; But[12] he whose heart is presumptuous in giving a judicial decision, is foolish, wicked and arrogant.

8. He used to say[13]: judge not alone, for none may judge alone save one. And say not "accept my view", for they are free but not you.

9. Rabbi Jonathan said[14]: whoever fulfills the Torah out of a state of poverty, his end will be to fulfill it out of a state of wealth; And whoever discards the torah out of a state of wealth, his end will be to discard it out of a state of poverty.

10. Rabbi Meir said[15]: Engage but little in business, and busy yourself with the Torah. Be of humble spirit

---

[12] **Rambam** - He is nonchalant in legal decisions to force his decisions without awe and fear.

[13] **Rambam** - The Torah permitted an expert known to the public to judge by himself, as we explained in Sanhedrin. But this is the word of the Torah and here it warns him a little from the angle of ethics and not from the angle of prohibition. And he said that if your colleagues disagree with you in an opinion from the opinions, do not force them to accept your argument - as they know if they must accept it, and it is not your right to force them to accept your opinion.

[14] **Rambam** - He said that anyone that is occupied with Torah and is poor and needy and - with all of this - pains himself to be occupied with it; in the end he will be occupied with it in wealth, such that there not be anything to disturb him from the reading. And one who is not occupied with Torah because of his multitude of money so that his involvement is in eating and in drinking and in rest; in the end he will become impoverished and time will be tight for him - until the reason for his neglect of the reading will be his preoccupation with bread for him to eat.

[15] **Rambam** - He said to minimize your business and be constant with the Torah and Be humble of spirit before everyone - meaning to say that you not be humble of spirit in front of the

before all men. If you have neglected the Torah, you shall have many who bring you to neglect it, but if you have labored at the study of Torah, there is much reward to give unto you

11. Rabbi Eliezer ben Jacob said: he who performs one commandment acquires[16] for himself one advocate, and he who commits one transgression acquires for himself one accuser. Repentance and good deeds are a shield against punishment. Rabbi Yochanan Hasandlar said: every assembly which is for the sake of heaven, will in the end endure; and every assembly which is not for the sake of heaven, will not endure in the end.

12. Rabbi Elazar ben Shammua said: let the honor of your student be as dear to you as your own, and the honor of your colleague as the reverence for your teacher, and the reverence for your teacher as the reverence of heaven.

---

big people alone; indeed, in front of every man. Such that when you sit with any man that it be, your speaking with him should be as if he is greater than you. And all of this is to flee from pride, as we have elucidated. And the matter of many reasons for neglecting it will be presented to you is that there are many things that cause neglect and require someone to be occupied with them. And when you are not occupied with Torah, time will disturb you with one of those things.

[16] **Rambam** - A praklit is efender, is a man that advises good for a person to the authorities. A katigor (prosecutor) is the opposite of this - and he is one who tale-bears on a man to the king and attempts to kill him. And they said that repentance after bad deeds or good deeds from the start - each of these two matters - prevent injuries and sicknesses from coming to a person.

PIRKI AVOT — Chapter 4 — Rambam

13. Rabbi Judah said[17]: be careful in study, for an error in study counts as deliberate sin. Rabbi Shimon said: There are three crowns: the crown of torah, the crown of priesthood, and the crown of royalty, but the crown of a good name supersedes them all.

14. Rabbi Nehorai said[18]: go as a voluntary exile to a place of Torah and say not that it will come after you, for it is your fellow students who will make it permanent in your hand and[19] "and lean not upon your own understanding".

15. Rabbi Yannai said[20]: it is not in our hands to explain the reason either of the security of the wicked, or even

---

[17] **Rambam** - These three good ranks were given to this nation at the beginning of the giving of the Torah. And they are priesthood, monarchy and Torah. Aharon merited to take priesthood, David merited to take monarchy, but the crown of Torah remains for anyone who wants to be crowned with it. And the rabbis, may their memory be blessed, said (Yoma 72b), "And lest you will say that this crown is less than the other two, it is not like that. Rather it is greater than both of them. And the two are in it, as it is stated (Proverbs 8:15), 'Through me kings reign and rulers decree just laws' and it states (Proverbs 8:16), 'Through me ministers administer, etc.'" But the crown of a good name comes from Torah as well, meaning to say its knowledge and its practice - as through them does a truly good name come.

[18] **Rambam** - He said to seek a proper place for reading and study, as the reading will become firm and be established when you are with another person. And do not rely upon your own understanding and say that you do not need colleagues and students that will stimulate you.

[19] Proverbs 3:5

[20] **Rambam** - He said that a man's being a student to someone who is wiser than he is better and more fit than being a teacher to someone lesser than he - as in the first situation he will gain and in the second situation he will decrease. And you should

of the afflictions of the righteous. Rabbi Mathia ben Harash said: Upon meeting people, be the first to extend greetings; And be a tail unto lions, and not a head unto foxes.

16. Rabbi Jacob said: this world is like a vestibule before the world to come; prepare yourself in the vestibule, so that you may enter[21] the banqueting-hall.

17. He used to say[22]: more precious is one hour in repentance and good deeds in this world, than all the

---

understand [it] from that which we elucidated in Sanhedrin, that they placed the head of an academy of twenty-three [scholars] at the back of a great academy of seventy-one, because of the principle that 'we bring up in holiness and we do not bring down' - as they saw that they raised his rank with this.

[21] **Rambam** - A traklin is a chamber and a prozdor is a gatehouse. And the metaphor is clear and the intention is known. As it is in this world that a man acquires the virtues through which he merits the world to come. As this world is indeed a path and a passageway to the world to come.

[22] **Rambam** - We have already elucidated in the tenth chapter of Sanhedrin that there is no completion or addition after death. Instead, a person increases and completes his virtue in this world. And about this Shlomo hinted when he stated (Ecclesiastes 9:10), "for there is no action, no reasoning, no knowledge, no wisdom in the grave to where you are going." But this matter is that the situation to which a person goes will remain the same forever. And because of this a man should make efforts during this short time and not waste his time, but only [spend it] on the acquisition of virtues - as his loss would otherwise be great, since he has no replacement for it and he cannot acquire it later. And since the pious ones knew this, they only saw fit to finish their time with wisdom and the increase of virtues; and they benefited from all of their time in the true way. And they only frittered very little time on physical matters and on a thing that it is necessary and impossible without it. But others spent all of their time only in physicality and they left the world like they came to

life of the world to come; And more precious is one hour of the tranquility of the world to come, than all the life of this world.

18. Rabbi Shimon ben Elazar said[23]: Do not try to appease your friend during his hour of anger; Nor comfort him at the hour while his dead still lies before him; Nor question him at the hour of his vow; Nor strive to see him in the hour of his disgrace.

19. Shmuel Hakatan said[24]: "If your enemy falls, do not exult; if he trips, let your heart not rejoice, lest the Lord see it and be displeased, and avert his wrath[25] from him".

---

it - 'all corresponding to how it came, so will it go' - and they lost an eternal loss. And the masses all switched the truth about this question and said that the first group lost the world and that the last group profited from the world. And the matter is the opposite, as we have recounted. And they make darkness into light and light into darkness. And woe is it to those that destroy the truth. And Shlomo, peace be upon him, made this matter a fundamental in Ecclesiastes, in his praising the profit of the world and his disgracing its loss. And its elucidation is that there is neither gain nor any other acquisition of that which he refrained from here, after death. And this is all true. And when you examine that book from this perspective, the truth will be clear.

[23] **Rambam** - This is clear and they are matters of ethics in the improvement of human society by the placement of a word in a place where it will be effective.

[24] Proverbs 24:17

[25] **Rambam** - 'The burning of His anger' is not stated which is only the heat of anger, but rather "His anger"; this teaches that he is forgiven for all of his sins: And even though Shlomo said this command in his wisdom first in Proverbs, this sage would teach this trait and warn about this sin.

PIRKI AVOT — Chapter 4 — Rambam

20. Elisha ben Abuyah said[26]: He who learns when a child, to what is he compared? To ink written upon a new writing sheet. And he who learns when an old man, to what is he compared? To ink written on a rubbed writing sheet. Rabbi Yose ben Judah a man of Kfar Hababli said: He who learns from the young, to what is he compared? To one who eats unripe grapes, and drinks wine from his vat; And he who learns from the old, to what is he compared? To one who eats ripe grapes, and drinks old wine. Rabbi said: don't look at the container but at that which is in it: there is a new container full of old wine, and an old container in which there is not even new wine.

21. Rabbi Elazar Ha-kappar said[27]: envy, lust and the desire for honor put a man out of the world.

---

[26] **Rambam** - He said that study during the days of childhood will be established and it will not be easily forgotten and that the matter of study in old age is the opposite. And this is clear and visible to the eye. Rabbi Yossi said that the wisdom of young men has questions and doubts that are not purified. And they have not escaped from their difficulties, as they have not had length of days to review their studies and to remove the doubts. But Rebbi says that you should not judge the wine by the jug. As there is a new jug with old wine in it and an old jug that is empty and has nothing in it. So too, there are young men whose questions and wisdom are pure - there is no doubt mixed with them - like old wine, the sediments of which have been separated from it. And there are elders that have no wisdom at all, and there is no need to say that they do not have wisdom that is mixed and confused.

[27] **Rambam** - He said that envy, lust and pursuit of honor drive a man form the world. And that is because these traits - or even just one of them - perforce destroy the faith of the Torah. And so, neither the intellectual virtues or the dispositional virtues will reach him.

PIRKI AVOT   Chapter 4   Rambam

22. He used to say[28]: the ones who were born are to die, and the ones who have died are to be brought to life,

---

[28] **Rambam** - He said, "to know, to make known, and to become conscious". He means with this that He knows the ones that will be born in the future, those that are born now and will die and those that will [return to life] after death. And we learn from these three groups that He is the Maker; He is the Creator. And with his saying, "He is the Judge… and He is destined to judge," he wants to say that He judges everything now with life and death and all of the other matters of the world, and He is also destined to judge those that will live in the world to come, for reward and punishment. And his saying, no taking of bribes, is like it also stated in the Torah (Deuteronomy 10:17), "shows no favor and takes no bribe." And its matter is not that He does not take a bribe to sway the judgement, as this is from idiocy which is distant from God, may He be blessed - such that it cannot be designed and cannot even be imagined. As how can a bribe be designed for Him - and what will the bribe be? Rather its matter is that which we have elucidated - that He not take the good deeds as a bribe. Such that if a man did a thousand good [deeds] and one evil, God, may He be blessed, will not forgive the one sin for the multitude of his good deeds and remove one or more goods from his thousand goods. Rather, He will punish for that one evil and reward him for all of those goods. And this is the matter of "takes no bribes." And it is like, "shows no favor" - that He punishes one great in virtues for a small thing; like our teacher Moshe, peace be upon him, was punished for the sin of anger, as we explained in previous chapters, and the reward of Esav the evildoer for honoring father and mother and of Nevuchadnetzar for the honor of God, may He be blessed, as it is clarified in Sanhedrin. And that is the matter of no respect of persons. And examine the statement, against your will you were created, and that which is connected to it - that he mentioned natural matters about which a man has no choice; about which the rabbis, may their memory be blessed, said (Berakhot 33b), "Everything is in the hands of Heaven except for the fear of Heaven." And he did not say, "Against your will you sin," or

and the ones brought to life are to be judged; So that one may know, make known and have the knowledge that He is God, He is the designer, He is the creator, He is the discerner, He is the judge, He the witness, He the complainant, and that He will summon to judgment. Blessed be He, before Whom there is no iniquity, nor forgetting, nor respect of persons, nor taking of bribes, for all is His. And know that all is according to the reckoning. And let not your impulse assure thee that the grave is a place of refuge for you; for against your will were you formed, against your will were you born, against your will you live, against your will you will die, and against your will you will give an account and reckoning before the King of the kings of kings, the Holy One, blessed be He.

"pass" or "go" or "stand" or what is similar to this. As these are all matters that are in the control of a man and about which there is no compulsion with them, as we explained in the fifth chapter (Eight Chapters 5).

Chapter 5

1. With[1] ten utterances the world was created. And what does this teach, for surely it could have been created with one utterance? But this was so in order to punish the wicked who destroy the world that was created with ten utterances. And to give a good reward to the righteous who maintain the world that was created with ten utterances.

2. Ten generations[2] There were from Adam to Noah, in order to make known what long-suffering is His; for all

---

[1] **Rambam** - With ten utterances: When you observe everything that comes in the story of creation, you will find, "and He said," nine times. And "In the beginning" is the tenth [utterance]. And even though the word, "and He said," does not elucidate this, the content indicates it. And it as if it said, "And God said, 'Let there be the heavens and the earth.'" As they could not have been without an utterance. And He could have spoken the entire creation with one utterance by saying, "And God said, 'Let there be the heavens and the earth and let there be the firmament and let the waters gather, etc.'" Instead, He designated a [separate] utterance for each matter, to make known the greatness of this existence and the goodness of its order; and that one who destroys it destroys something great and that one who refines it refines something great. He means to say that the one who destroys his soul - which is in his hand to refine or to destroy - destroys [the world]; since it is as if he is the final purpose from all of existence, for which He said ten utterances - as we elucidated in the introduction of this essay of ours.

[2] **Rambam** - These generations are the words of the Torah, "x begot y," according to its order. And it mentioned this and that which is after it because of its mentioning [the] ten utterances, which has reproach in them for man; to arouse him and to refine

those generations kept on provoking Him, until He brought upon them the waters of the flood. [There were] ten generations from Noah to Abraham, in order to make known what long-suffering is His; for all those generations kept on provoking Him, until Abraham, came and received the reward of all of them.

3. With[3] ten trials was Abraham, our father may he rest in peace, tried, and he withstood them all; to make known how great was the love of Abraham, our father peace be upon him.

---

his soul with the dispositional virtues and the intellectual virtues, which is the intention of this tractate.

[3] **Rambam** - The ten tests with which Abraham, our father, was tested are all [in] the words of Scripture. The first is his emigration by His statement, may He be blessed - "Go forth from your land, etc." (Genesis 12:1). And the second one is the famine that was found in the Land of Canaan when he came there and it was [the land of] his destiny - "and I will make you into a great nation" (Genesis 12:2). And this was a great test, and it is its saying, "And there was a famine in the land" (Genesis 12:10). And the third was the injustice of the Egyptians towards him in the taking of Sarah to Pharaoh. The fourth is his fighting against the four kings. The fifth is his taking of Hagar as a wife after he despaired of giving birth through Sarah. The sixth is the circumcision that he was commanded about in the days of his old age. The seventh is the injustice of the king of Gerar towards him in his also taking Sarah. The eighth is the expulsion of Hagar after his being built (having a child) from her. The ninth is the distancing of his son, Yishmael, and that is His, may He be blessed, saying, "Let not it be bad in your eyes about the youth, etc." (Genesis 21:12). And Scripture already testified how this thing was difficult in his eyes, in its stating, "And the thing was very bad in the eyes of Abraham" (Genesis 21:11). Yet he observed the commandment of God, may He be blessed, and expelled him. And the tenth is the binding of Yitzchak.

PIRKI AVOT — Chapter 1 — Rambam

4. Ten[4] miracles were wrought for our ancestors in Egypt, and ten at the sea. Ten plagues did the Holy one,

---

[4] **Rambam** - But the ten miracles that were performed for our ancestors in Egypt are their salvation from the ten plagues and that each of the ten plagues were specifically on the Egyptians and not on Israel. And these are miracles without a doubt. And the language of the Torah in each and every plague is that the Holy One, blessed be He, brought it [only] on the Egyptians. Except for the plague of lice - as [there] it did not make this clear, but it is known that He did not punish Israel. Rather [the lice] were found with [the Israelites as well], but they did not distress them. And so did the sages elucidate. But with the other plagues, the matter was clarified [in the text]. It stated about the blood (Exodus 7:21), "and the Egyptians could not drink water from the river" - a proof that that the damage reached them alone. And it stated with the frogs (Exodus 7:28), "and they will come into your house and into your bedrooms, etc." And it stated with the mixture of animals (Exodus 8:18), "And I will distinguish on that day the Land of Goshen, etc." And it stated about the pestilence (Exodus 9:6), "but of the livestock of the Israelites not one died." And it sated about the boils (Exodus 9:11), "as the boils were upon the magicians and and upon all of Egypt." And it stated with the hail (Exodus 9:26), "Only in the Land of Goshen, where the Israelites were, there was no hail." And it stated with the locusts (Exodus 10:14), "And locusts went up upon all the Land of Egypt." And it stated with darkness (Exodus 10:23), "and for all the children of Israel, there was light in their dwellings." But the ten miracles that were at the Sea is a received tradition. The first is the splitting of the water like the simple understanding of the verse, "and the water split" (Exodus 14:21). The second is that after the sea split, it became like a tent until it turned into a type of roof - and not of beams and not slanted - and the path was as if there was a hole in the water and the water was on the right and on the left and on top. It is [like] the statement of Habakuk 3:14, "You have pierced with his rods, the head of his rulers." The third is that its ground became hard and solid, as it states (Exodus 14:29), "walked on dry land" - and there did not

remain any clay and mud like in other rivers. The fourth is that the paths of the Egyptians were in quicksand, and that is its stating (Habakuk 3:14), "the clay of great waters." The fifth is that it split into twelve paths like the number of tribes like a curved bow, as per this drawing. And that is its stating (Psalms 136:13), "To tear the Reed Sea into pieces." The sixth is that the water congealed and became as hard as boulders. And about this, it stated (Psalms 74:13), "you broke the head of the 'sea monsters' upon the waters" - meaning to say that the waters hardened to the point that they went back in such a way that heads would break on them. And the seventh is that it did not congeal like the solidifying of other waters that congeal - meaning to say [into] one piece, but rather [into] many pieces, as if they were [building] stones and they were arranged some on top of others. And that is its stating (Psalms 74:13), "You crumbled the sea with Your power." The eighth is that it congealed like glass or onyx - meaning to say, it was clear to the point that some of [the tribes] would see each other in their crossing it. And this is its stating (Psalms 18:12), "the darkness of the waters, the clouds of the sky," which is to say that the gathering of waters was 'like the essence of the sky in purity' - which is clear. The ninth - that sweet water would flow from it and they would drink it. The tenth is that it would congeal at the time that it flowed, after they took what they drank from it - to the point that it would not fall to the ground. And that is its stating (Exodus 15:8), "they stood up like a flowing stack" - meaning to say the thing that was flowing congealed in the heart of the sea. And in the tradition we found that more plagues came upon the Egyptians at the Sea than the plagues that came upon them in Egypt. And the hint to this is in its stating (I Samuel 4:8), "He is the same God who struck the Egyptians with every plague in the wilderness" - meaning to say in the Wilderness of the Reed Sea. But the ten trials that our ancestors tested the Omnipresent are all words of Scripture. The first is at the Sea in their saying "Are there no graves in Egypt" (Exodus 14:11). And the second is at Marah - that is its stating (Exodus 15:24), "And they complained about Moshe, saying, 'What will we drink?'" And the third is in the Wilderness of Sin

blessed be He, bring upon the Egyptians in Egypt and ten at the sea. With ten trials did our ancestors try God, blessed be He, as it is said[5], "and they have tried Me these ten times and they have not listened to my voice".
5. Ten wonders were wrought for our ancestors in the Temple: **1-** no woman miscarried from the odor of the sacred flesh; **2-** the sacred flesh never became putrid; **3-** no fly was ever seen in the slaughterhouse; **4-** no emission occurred to the high priest on the Day of Atonement; **5-** the[6] rains did not extinguish the fire of

---

when they asked for the manna. And that is its stating (Exodus 16:3), "And who will give that our death be at the hand of God, etc." And the fourth is their leaving manna over until the morning. And that is its stating (Exodus 16:20), "and men left over from it until the morning." And the fifth is their rebellion in seeking manna on the Shabbat day, as it is stated (Exodus 16:27), "And it was on the seventh day some of the people went out to gather." And the sixth is their rebellion at Refidim, also over water. And the seventh is at Chorev with the story of the [golden] calf. And the eighth is at Taverah when they become doubtful at that place with the speaking of the grumblers. And that is its saying (Numbers 11:1), "And the people were like grumblers." And the ninth is at Kivrot HaTaavah (the graves of desire), when they asked for meat - its saying (Numbers 11:4), "And the mixed multitude that was within them desired a desire." And the tenth is in the Wilderness of Paran with the matter of the spies. And there it stated (Numbers 14:22), "and they have tried Me these ten times and they did not listen to My voice."
[5] Numbers 14:22
[6] **Rambam** - You already know that the altar was in the middle of the courtyard - and we will elucidate this in the future in its place - and it was open to the skies. And with all of this, the rains did not extinguish the fire of the wood pile. And the wind did not dissipate the pillar of smoke that arose from the sacrifices. Rather, the air during the time of the sacrificing was fresh. And

PIRKI AVOT Chapter 1 Rambam

the woodpile; **6-** the wind did not prevail against the column of smoke; **7-** no defect was found in the omer, or in the two loaves, or in the showbread; **8-** the people stood pressed together, yet bowed down and had room enough; **9-** never did a serpent or a scorpion harm anyone in Jerusalem; **10-** and no man said to his fellow: the place is too congested for me to lodge overnight in Jerusalem.

6. Ten things were created on the eve of the Sabbath at twilight, and these are they: **1-** the mouth of the earth; **2-** the mouth of the well; **3-** the mouth of the donkey; **4-** the rainbow; **5-** the manna; **6-** the staff of Moses; **7-** the shamir; **8-** the letters; **9-** the writing, **10-** and the tablets. And some say: also, the demons, the grave of Moses, and the ram of Abraham, our father. And some say: and also, tongs[7], made with tongs.

---

they would stand in the courtyard one next to another; but at the time of bowing down, they did not push against one another, due to their great awe and tranquility in this place.

[7] **Rambam** - Also the [first human-made] tongs, made with [Divine] tongs: [As] who made the first ones? We have already mentioned in the eighth chapter (Eight Chapters 8:9-10) that they would not believe in creation by the (Divine) will at every instant. Rather, at the beginning of things, He placed into [their] nature that they should do everything that they would do [in the future] - whether they be things that would happen constantly, that being a natural thing; or whether it be [something unusual], that being a miracle. It is all one [regarding this]. Therefore they said that on the sixth day, He placed into the nature of the earth that it would sink [under] Korach and his community, and into the well that it would give out water and into the donkey that it should speak, and so [too] for the rest. And ketav (letters) is the Torah that was written in front of Him, may He be blessed, as it is stated. And we do not know how it was - and that is its stating

PIRKI AVOT   Chapter 1   Rambam

7. Seven things there are characteristic in a clod, and seven in a wise man[8]: **A** wise man does not speak before

---

(Exodus 24:12), "and I will give you the stone tablets." And the miktav (writing) is the writing on the tablets, as it stated (Exodus 32:16), "and the writing was God's writing, inscribed upon the tablets." And maybe you will say [that] since all of the wonders are all placed into the nature of things from the six days of creation, why did he distinguish these ten things. You should [hence] know that he did not distinguish these ten things to say that no other miracle was placed into the nature of things except for these. Rather, he said that these alone were done at twilight and the rest of the wonders and miracles were placed into the nature of things that they were put into at the time of their original creation. And they said by way of example that [on] the second day in the division of the waters, it was placed into the nature [of water] that the Reed Sea would divide for Moshe, and that the Jordan would divide for Yehoshua and also for Eliyahu and also for Elisha. And [on] the fourth day when the sun was created, it was placed into its nature that it would stop at time x by the word of Yehoshua to it. And so [too] with the other wonders except for these ten that were put into the nature of these things at twilight. And the shamir is a small creeping thing that chisels big stones when it goes on top of them, and Shlomo built the Temple with it. And tongs are a tool with which the blacksmith holds the hot iron until he makes what he wants to make with it.

[8] **Rambam** - Behold I will first explain these character [types] that are frequently repeated in the words of the sages. And they are the boor (buur), the ignoramus (am ha'arets), the unformed person (golem), the wise man and the pious man. Indeed, a buur (literally, an empty pit) is a man that does not have intellectual virtues nor dispositional virtues - meaning to say, neither wisdom nor ethics. And he also does not have acquisition of knowledge - [it is] as if he is naked of the good and of the bad. And he is called buur to compare him to land that is not sown with anything, and that is called a sdeh buur (empty field), as it is explained in [the Order of] Seeds (Zeraim). And an am ha'arets

PIRKI AVOT — Chapter 1 — Rambam

is a man that has dispositional virtues but he does not have intellectual virtues - meaning to say that he has [knowledge] of the ways of the world (derekh erets) but does not have Torah in his hand. And he is called an am ha'arets (literally, people of the land), meaning to say that he is good for the settling of the land and the societies of the states, since he has dispositional virtues through which he will connect well with others - as we explained in the beginning of our essay. And an unformed person is a man that has intellectual virtues and dispositional virtues. However, they are not complete and properly organized. Rather, they have clutter and confusion and there is a lack mixed in with them. And because of this, he is called a golem - to compare him to a tool that a craftsman has made that has the [initial] form of [its] function [but] is missing its completion and refinement. [An example of this is] a knife and a sword that the blacksmith has made not [completely] formed, and their form comes to them before they sand them and sharpen them and smoothen them and engrave whatever is their way to engrave upon them and complete its refinement. And before this, they are called golmei (initial forms of) tools of metals, as it is explained in Kelim (Mishnah Kelim 12:6). And it is a Hebrew word: "My unformedness (golmi) Your eyes saw" (Psalms 139:16) - meaning to say, my substance before the form of the man came to it. And when this form does not reach its completion, they called it a golem, to compare it to substance that is designed to receive a different form through which it will become more complete. And a wise man is one to which these two types of virtues have come to completeness, as is needed. And a pious man is the wise one when he has added to [his] virtue, meaning to say to the dispositional virtues, to the point that he inclines a little towards one of the extremes - as we have explained in the fourth chapter (Eight Chapters 4:7). And [so] his deeds will be greater than his wisdom. And because of this supplement, he is a called a pious man (chassid). As the increase of something is called chessed - whether that increase is for good or for evil. And he said here that the wise man will have these seven virtues, and they are great fundamentals. And because of that, he focuses on

PIRKI AVOT   Chapter 1   Rambam

them - as through them analysis and study and [proper] action are possible. And four of them are dispositional virtues. And they are that he does not speak in front of someone who is greater than him in wisdom; and he does not interrupt the words of his fellow - but he desists until he finishes his words; and he does not bluster about what he does not know, and that is his saying "about that which he has not heard [anything], he says, 'I have not heard [anything]'"; and he is not stubborn, but when he hears the truth, he concedes to it - and even about that which he is able to refute and to disagree with and to misconstrue, he does not want to do it - and this is his saying, "and he concedes to the truth". And [the following are] the three intellectual virtues: [The first is] that when a deceiver deceives him with his rhetoric of deception, he should not be impulsive and remain in doubt about the truth. Rather, he should quickly sense the source of the error and clarify it. And this is his saying, "and is not impulsive in answering." And this is actually from ease of comprehension and proper examination of the deceiver's argument to understand the difference in the words. And the second virtue is that he asks what needs to be asked about that matter - and he does not ask for a logical proof in natural science, nor for a scientific argument in the wisdoms of logic and similar to this. And if he is the one asked, he should also answer according to the category of the question. If he is asked about matters the nature of which is that they can be proven, he should answer from the category of the inquirer with a proof; and if he is asked about that which is lower than this, he should answer according to its science and [style] of proof. And he should also not be asked about a material explanation and give a formal explanation or be asked about a formal explanation and give a material explanation. But rather he answers according to the purpose. And this is his saying, "he asks to the point and answers as is proper." And the third virtue is that he organizes his study and puts first what is fitting to put first and puts later what is fitting to put later. As this approach is very helpful in study. And that is his saying, "he speaks to the first [point] first and the last [point] last." And all of these are the

PIRKI AVOT   Chapter 1   Rambam

one who is greater than he in wisdom, And does not break into his fellow's speech; And is not hasty to answer; He asks what is relevant, and he answers to the point; And he speaks of the first [point] first, and of the last [point] last; And concerning that which he has not heard, he says: I have not heard; And he acknowledges the truth. And the reverse of these are characteristic in a clod.

8. Seven kinds of punishment come to the world for seven categories of transgression: When some of them give tithes, and others do not give tithes, a[9] famine from drought comes some go hungry, and others are satisfied. When they have all decided not to give tithes, a famine from tumult and drought comes; When they have, in addition, decided] not to set apart the dough-offering, an all-consuming famine comes. Pestilence comes to the world for sins punishable by death according to the Torah, but which have not been referred to the court, and for neglect of the law regarding the fruits of the sabbatical year. The sword comes to the world for the delay[10] of judgment, and for

---

opposite with the unformed person, since he is not complete - as we have explained - and he has not reached this level.

[9] **Rambam** - A famine from drought is that the year be with little rain. It rains in some places and in some places it does not rain; and when it does rain, the rain will be little. And a famine from tumult is when a man is involved in wars and arguments and other novelties that come up for them until the land is unworked - and he does not plant at the time of planting from the [instability in] the world. And a famine of annihilation is that it not rains at all and the rivers and lakes dry up, as its stating (Deuteronomy 28:23), "And the skies above your head shall be copper."

[10] **Rambam** - Delay of justice is the postponement of judgement and its investigation for many days about something that is

the perversion of judgment, and because of those who teach the Torah not in accordance with the accepted law.

9. Wild beasts come to the world for swearing in vain, and for the profanation of the Name. Exile comes to the world for idolatry, for sexual sins and for bloodshed, and for transgressing the commandment of the year of the release of the land. At[11] four times pestilence increases: in the fourth year, in the seventh year and at the conclusion of the seventh year, and at the conclusion of the Feast of Tabernacles in every year. In the fourth year, on account of the tithe of the poor which is due in the third year. In the seventh year, on account of the tithe of the poor which is due in the sixth year; At the conclusion of the seventh year, on account of the produce of the seventh year; And at the conclusion of the Feast of Tabernacles in every year, for robbing the gifts to the poor.

---

already clear. And perversion of justice is when he judges in [a way] that is not proper.

[11] **Rambam** - We have already explained the order of the extraction of the obligations from produce many times in the Order of Seeds (Zeraim). And there it was clairified that in the third and sixth year, he would extract the first tithe and give it to the Levite [like] in each [and every] year. And afterwards, he would extract the poor tithe and give it to the poor. And this poor tithe was in place of the second tithe, which he would extract in other years of the sabbatitcal cycle. And the gifts to the poor are the gleanings, the produce that is forgotten, the produce that is in the corner of the field, the fallen grapes and the single strands of grapes. As at the holiday (Sukkot), they are all present - since occupation with the earth (agricultural pursuits) is already finished. And the one that gave these obligations, gave them; and the one who did not give them, stole them.

10. There[12] are four types of character in human beings: One that says: "mine is mine, and yours is yours": this is a commonplace type; and some say this is a sodom-type of character. One that says: "mine is yours and yours is mine": is an unlearned person (am haaretz); One that says: "mine is yours and yours is yours" is a pious person. One that says: "mine is mine, and yours is mine" is a wicked person.

11. There[13] are four kinds of temperament's: Easy to become angry, and easy to be appeased: his gain disappears in his loss; Hard to become angry, and hard to be appeased: his loss disappears in his gain; Hard to become angry and easy to be appeased: a pious person; Easy to become angry and hard to be appeased: a wicked person.

12. There[14] are four types of disciples: Quick to comprehend, and quick to forget: his gain disappears in

---

[12] **Rambam** - Behold it is elucidated in this statement that the pious one is one who multiplies good deeds - meaning to say that he inclines a little towards one of the two extremes. And it is also elucidated for you that one who has vices of the soul is called evil - meaning to say that he inclines towards the extreme that is extraneous, as we have explained in the fourth chapter (Eight Chapters 4). As the one who wants that he should have his money and the money of someone else has much desire and he is called evil.

[13] **Rambam** - Observe how he called the patient one, whose patience is excessive to the point that he approaches lack of feeling concerning the matter of anger, a pious man. And he called someone with the vices of the trait of anger, evil.

[14] **Rambam** - Observe how he did not call the one that is quick [and] has a good memory a pious one, because this is an intellectual virtue. And [so] he called him a wise man. And he did not call the one who has difficulty understanding matters and

his loss; Slow to comprehend, and slow to forget: his loss disappears in his gain; Quick to comprehend, and slow to forget: he is a wise man; Slow to comprehend, and quick to forget, this is an evil portion.

13. There[15] are four types of charity givers. He who wishes to give, but that others should not give: his eye is evil to that which belongs to others; He who wishes that others should give, but that he himself should not give: his eye is evil towards that which is his own; He who desires that he himself should give, and that others should give: he is a pious man; He who desires that he himself should not give and that others too should not give: he is a wicked man.

14. There[16] are four types among those who frequent the study-house (bet midrash): He who attends but does not practice: he receives a reward for attendance. He who practices but does not attend: he receives a reward for practice. He[17] who attends and practices: he is a pious

---

forgets much, evil - as it is not in his hand (control). And these are not virtues which are possible to acquire - as we explained in the second chapter (Eight Chapters 2:2).

[15] **Rambam** - Observe how he called one with so much mercy that he does not suffice that he alone should have mercy, but only that others should also have mercy, a pious man. And he called a cruel one, evil.

[16] **Rambam** - His saying, "among those who go to the House of Study," meaning to say, in the going to the House of Study, there are four traits. Observe how he called the one that proliferates acquisition of virtues a pious man, and the one who is lazy in their acquisition, evil.

[17] **Rambam** - And when you know the intellectual virtues and the dispositional virtues; and you know every type of them - if you want, study of wisdom and practice - and you know the mean and the ways of deeds that can be called good; and [know] the

PIRKI AVOT Chapter 1 Rambam

slight supplement to the mean which is from the famous actions of the pious ones; and [when you] know the supplement and the lack which are both bad -- just that one of them is more fit to [be called] evil and the other is called a transgression or an incorrect action, and the example with this is that caution is completely good without a doubt and much desire is completely bad without a doubt and the lack of feeling for enjoyment is actually not like much desire even though it is [also] bad and [so] it is called a transgression or an incorrect action, [such that] leaving caution slightly towards the side of lack of feeling is fit for the complete ones - and when you understand this matter, you will know that one who leaves caution slightly is called pious as we prefaced and that the lack of feeling is called a transgression, and that is why it stated about the nazirite (Numbers 6:11), "from that which he transgressed upon the soul," as we explained in the fourth chapter (Eight Chapters 4); and [when you understand] all of what we have prefaced and elucidated, you will know which [person] from among people is fitting to be called a boor and who is fitting to be called an ignoramus and who is fitting to be called and unformed person and who is fitting to be called a wise man and who is fitting to be called evil and who is fitting to be called a sinner. These seven names apply to seven people according to their having from the virtues and the vices and their study of the intellectual [virtues], as per what has come earlier in our commentary. And they already [added] names according to the properties of a man, as with the man who has vices in his traits - and he is called evil, as we have explained - but if he [also] has intellectual virtues that he uses for evil things, such a one is called by the sages a clever evildoer. And if he is an evildoer who hurts people - meaning to say that among his character vices are matters that hurt people, like brazenness and cruelty and [traits] similar to them - such a one is called a bad evildoer. And so [too] the one who has intellectual virtues and dispositional vices is called a wise man to do evil, as it states in the verse about someone like this (Jeremiah 4:22), "they are wise men to do evil; but to do good, they do not know" - meaning to say that they use their intellectual virtues for bad actions and not for good actions.

man; He who neither attends nor practices: he is a wicked man.

But the man who has all of the virtues gathered in him - the intellectual [ones] and the dispositional virtues - to the point that there is no intellectual virtue and no dispositional virtue not in him, and this is rarely found and the philosophers would say that finding such a person is very unlikely but not impossible and when they find him, they would call him a Godly man. And so [too], the sages called him in our language a man of God. And I say that this man is called an angel of the Lord, as it stated (Judges 2:1), "And the angel of the Lord went up from Gilgal." And the philosophers have said that it is impossible to find a man that has all of the vices gathered in him to their very end without intellectual [virtues] or ones of disposition to the point that he does not have virtue at all. And if one is found and this is improbable, they give him the name, 'an animal from the bad, dangerous animals.' And so [too] did Shlomo call him, a 'bereaved bear,' which is the gathering of stupidity and damage. And [of] these five compound names, four of them are to disparage - and they are the clever evildoer, the bad evildoer, the wise man to do evil and the bereaved bear - and one is for greatness, and there is nothing greater than it - and that is the man of God or the angel of the Lord. And Scripture has already elucidated that a man that has all of the intellectual and dispositional virtues found in him is called an angel of the Lord, and that is its stating (Malachi 2:7), "For the lips of a priest guard knowledge, and they seek Torah from his mouth; for he is an angel of the Lord of Hosts." And knowledge includes all of the intellectual virtues, as he will not be complete without them. And its stating, "they seek Torah from his mouth," is a proof of his completeness in dispositional virtues - as we have explained in the fourth chapter (Eight Chapters 4), that it is the intention of the Torah. And for [this reason], it states (Proverbs 3:17), "and all of its ways are peace." And we have already elucidated there (Eight Chapters 4) that peace is also from the dispositional virtues. And after [these indications of his completeness in the verse in Malachi], it stated, "for he is angel of the Lord of Hosts."

PIRKI AVOT — Chapter 1 — Rambam

15. There[18] are four types among those who sit before the sages: a sponge, a funnel, a strainer and a sieve. A sponge, soaks up everything; A funnel, takes in at one end and lets out at the other; A strainer, which lets out the wine and retains the lees; A sieve, which lets out the coarse meal and retains the choice flour.

16. All[19] love that depends on a something, when the thing ceases, the love ceases; and all love that does not depend on anything, will never cease. What is an example of love that depended on a something? Such was the love of Amnon for Tamar. And what is an example of love that did not depend on anything? Such was the love of David and Jonathan.

---

[18] **Rambam** - He compared the man with a good memory who remembers all that he hears and does not separate between the true and the false to a sponge - and that is a sea sponge that absorbs everything. And he also compared one who understands immediately but does not remember anything at all - not the true and not what is not true - to a funnel. And he compared one who ramblers the bad things and the opinion that is not true and forgets the true things upon which action [needs to be based] to a strainer that only retains the sediment and lets out what is pure. And he compared the man whose way is the opposite [of this] to a sieve that lets out the dirt and dust through its holes and the fine flour remains. And from them, only this fine flour sieve is good, in that it lets out the [inferior flour] that has no purpose and holds what is coarser - and that is the fine flour.

[19] **Rambam** - The explanation of these words is like this: You know that if the physical causes are negated and removed, then it will be necessary that what they cause will be removed with the removal of its cause. And because of this, when the cause of the love is a divine matter - and that is the true science - it is impossible for that love to be removed ever, as its cause is eternally in existence.

17. Every dispute that is for the sake of Heaven, will in the end endure; But one that is not for the sake of Heaven, will not endure. Which is the controversy that is for the sake of Heaven? Such was the controversy of Hillel and Shammai. And which is the controversy that is not for the sake of Heaven? Such was the controversy of Korah and all his congregation.

18. Whoever[20] causes the multitudes to be righteous, sin will not occur on his account; And whoever causes the multitudes to sin, they do not give him the ability to repent. Moses was righteous and caused the multitudes to be righteous. therefore, the righteousness of the multitudes is hung on him, as it is said[21], "He executed the Lord's righteousness and His decisions with Israel". Jeroboam, sinned and caused the multitudes to sin, therefore the sin of the multitudes is hung on him, as it is said[22], "For the sins of Jeroboam which he sinned, and which he caused Israel to sin thereby".

19. Whoever possesses these three things, he is of the disciples of Abraham, our father; and whoever possesses three other things, he is of the disciples of

---

[20] **Rambam** - This is all clear, as these matters are from the angle of reward and punishment. So that anyone who disagrees not with the intention to contradict the words of his fellow but from his wanting to know the truth, his words will endure and not end. And anyone who makes people straight, God, may He be blessed, will reward him by preventing him from transgression. And anyone who deceives people, God, may He be blessed, will punish him by preventing him from repentance. And this is clear and there is no difficulty in it, if you understand what we have outlined in the eighth chapter (Eight Chapters 8:14-16).

[21] Deuteronomy 33:21

[22] Kings-1 15:30

PIRKI AVOT   Chapter 1   Rambam

Balaam, the wicked. A[23] good eye, a humble spirit and a moderate appetite he is of the disciples of Abraham,

---

[23] **Rambam** - A good eye: We have explained many times that the matter of a good eye is sufficing and [that] a small appetite is carefulness and [that] a humble spirit is extreme humility as was explained in the chapter before this one (Rambam on Pirkei Avot 4:4). And the three [negative traits] that correspond to them are zeal to acquire money and that is an evil eye, and much desire and that is a broad appetite and arrogance and that is a haughty spirit. And these three virtues are publicized in Abraham, our father. And because of this, anyone who is found to have these virtues is called one of the students of Abraham, our father - as he followed his traits. And anyone within whom is found these three vices is of the students of Bilaam the evildoer - as he followed his traits. And I will mention the places in which are elucidated these virtues in Abraham and these vices in Bilaam, and they are all found in the Torah. Indeed, the sufficing of Abraham is in his saying to the king of Sedom (Genesis 14:23), "If from a thread to a sandal strap, and if I take from any of what is yours, etc." And that is the epitome of sufficing - that a man leaves much money and not benefit from it, even a little bit. But his caution is his saying to Sarah on the day they came to Egypt (Genesis 12:11), "Behold, I have known that you are a woman of beautiful appearance." And the explanation comes that he did not fully look at her form besides that day - and that is the epitome of carefulness. And [it is also shown] in his saying about Hagar after he married her (Genesis 16:6), " Behold, your maidservant is in your hands - do to her as is good in your eyes." [This] shows that he did not wish to enjoy himself with her. And so [too] when Sarah requested from him to expel her with Yishmael such that he would be prevented from inclining towards [Hagar] for sexual matters, the verse testifies that it was only bad in his eyes about Yishmael, and that is its stating (Genesis 21:11), "And the matter was very bad in the eyes of Abraham on account of his son." These are all signs of carefulness. And, indeed, his humility is his stating (Genesis 18:27), "and I am dust and ashes." And Bilaam the evildoer's zeal

our father. An evil eye, a haughty spirit and a limitless appetite he is of the disciples of Balaam, the wicked. What is the difference between the disciples of Abraham, our father, and the disciples of Balaam, the wicked? The disciples of Abraham, our father, enjoy this world, and inherit the world to come, as it is said[24]:

---

for money was publicized and that is his coming from Aram Naharaim for the sake of the money with which he was hired to curse Israel. And that is His, may He be blessed, stating (Deuteronomy 23:5), "since he hired against you Balaam son of Beor, etc." And, indeed, his great desire in sexual matters is the reason for his advice to Balak that he set loose the women to be promiscuous with [the men of] Israel and to place known harlots [in front of them]. As were it not for the great desire that he had and that harlots were good in his eyes, he would not have commanded this - since the commands of people are only according to their opinions. As the good will not command to [do] evil, but will rather warn against it. And the language of Scripture (Numbers 31:16) is "They are the very ones against the children of Israel by the word of Bilaam, etc." And the sages said (Sanhedrin 105a) [that] Bilaam had sexual relations with his donkey. And there is no doubt about it that one with such an opinion will have actions [like] this. And indeed, his arrogance is his stating (Numbers 24:16), "Speaks the one who hears the words of God." And indeed that which it brought a proof about Bilaam from its stating (Psalms 55:24), "And You, God, will bring them down to the pit of destruction; the people of blood, etc." - [its] explanation is [that it is] because he was a man of blood - as he was the cause of the Israelites' death in the plague; and he was also a man of deceit in his creating a machination to bring about the evil. And its bringing a proof about the students of Abraham from its stating (Proverbs 8:21), "There is what for those that love Me to inherit, and their treasuries will I fill" is like that which He called him (Isaiah 41:8), "the seed of Abraham, the one I love."

[24] Proverbs 8:21

PIRKI AVOT — Chapter 1 — Rambam

"I will endow those who love me with substance, I will fill their treasuries". But the disciples of Balaam, the wicked, inherit gehinnom, and descend into the nethermost pit, as it is said[25]: "For you, O God, will bring them down to the nethermost pit those murderous and treacherous men; they shall not live out half their days; but I trust in You".

20. Judah ben Tema said[26]: Be strong as a leopard, and swift as an eagle, and fleet as a gazelle, and brave as a lion, to do the will of your Father who is in heaven. He used to say: the arrogant is headed for Gehinnom and the blushing for the garden of Eden. May it be the will, O Lord our God, that your city be rebuilt speedily in our days and set our portion in the studying of your Torah.

---

[25] Psalms 55:24

[26] **Rambam** - Even though he said, "[the] brazen-faced [are bound] for Gehinnom (Purgatory), he commanded brazenness in the rebuke of rebels and similar to it. And it is as if he said, "Use a little of the vices in their [correct] place for the will of God, may He be blessed, and His truth." [And it is] like the statement of the prophet (II Samuel 22:27), "and with the perverse, you are wily." However, it is on condition that your intention is the truth; and that is the meaning of his saying, "to do the Will of your Father Who is in Heaven." And from the good things that God, may He be blessed, did for this nation is that they are shamefaced. And so [too], they said (Yevamot 79a) that the signs of the seed of Avraham is that they are shamefaced, merciful and doers of kindnesses. And it stated (Exodus 20:17), "so that My awe be upon your faces, that you not sin." And when he told about the virtues of shame, he requested and said, "Lord, our God - [just] like You have graced us with this virtue, so [too] grace us that Your city be rebuilt, speedily and in our days."

21. He used to say: At five years of age the study of Scripture; At ten the study of Mishnah; At thirteen subject to the commandments; At fifteen the study of Talmud; At eighteen the bridal canopy; At twenty for pursuit [of livelihood]; At thirty the peak of strength; At forty wisdom; At fifty able to give counsel; At sixty old age; At seventy fullness of years; At eighty the age of "strength"; At ninety a bent body; At one hundred, as good as dead and gone completely out of the world.

22. Ben Bag Bag said: Turn[27] it over, and [again] turn it over, for all is therein. And look into it; And become gray and old therein; And do not move away from it, for you have no better portion than it.

23. Ben He He said[28]: According to the labor is the reward.

---

[27] **Rambam** - He said about the Torah that one should search in it and meditate upon it, as everything is in it. And he said, "And in it should you see (techezei)," meaning to say the truth. [The explanation is that] you will see the truth with the eye of the intellect, like the [Aramaic] translation of vayira (and he saw) is vechaza. And afterwards he said, "and grow old and be worn in it" - to say, occupy yourself with it until the time of old age; and even then, do not veer from it to something else.

[28] **Rambam** - And Ben Hey Hey said [that] according to that which you are in pain with Torah will be your reward. And they said that only that which you study with exertion, labor and fear from the teacher will endure; but reading of enjoyment and leisure has no endurance to it and [so] no point in it. And they said in the explanation of his statement (Ecclesiastes 2:9), "even (af, which can also be understood as anger) my wisdom remained with me" - the wisdom that I studied with anger remained with me. And because of this, they commanded to place fear upon the students; and they said (Ketuvot 103b), "Throw fear upon the students."

Chapter 6

1. The[1] sages taught in the language of the Mishnah. Blessed be He who chose them and their teaching. Rabbi Meir said: Whoever occupies himself with the Torah for its own sake, merits many things; not only that but he is worth the whole world. He is called beloved friend; one that loves God; one that loves humankind; one that gladdens God; one that gladdens humankind. And the Torah clothes him in humility and reverence, and equips him to be righteous, pious, upright and trustworthy; it keeps him far from sin, and brings him near to merit. And people benefit from his counsel, sound knowledge, understanding and strength, as it is said[2], "Counsel is mine and sound wisdom; I am understanding, strength is mine". And it bestows upon him royalty, dominion, and acuteness in judgment. To him are revealed the secrets of the Torah, and he is made as an ever-flowing spring, and like a stream that never ceases. And he becomes modest, long-suffering and forgiving of insult. And it magnifies him and exalts him over everything.

2. Rabbi Joshua ben Levi said: every day a bat kol - a heavenly voice goes forth from Mount Horeb and makes proclamation and says: "Woe unto humankind for their contempt towards the Torah", for whoever does not occupy himself with the study of Torah is

---

[1] The Rambam did not have any commentary on this chapter. This chapter was written after the Mishnah was completed. The chapter begins with this part: The sages taught in the language of the Mishnah.

[2] Proverbs 8:14

called, nazuf the rebuked. As it is said[3], "Like a gold ring in the snout of a pig is a beautiful woman bereft of sense". And it says[4], "And the tablets were the work of God, and the writing was the writing of God, graven upon the tablets". Read not haruth - 'graven' but heruth - 'freedom'. For there is no free man but one that occupies himself with the study of the Torah. And whoever regularly occupies himself with the study of the Torah he is surely exalted, as it is said[5], "And from Mattanah to Nahaliel; and Nahaliel to Bamoth".

3. One who learns from his fellow one chapter, or one halakhah, or one verse, or one word, or even one letter, is obligated to treat him with honor; for so we find with David, king of Israel, who learned from Ahitophel no more than two things, yet called him his master, his guide and his beloved friend, as it is said[6], "But it was you, a man mine equal, my guide and my beloved friend". Is this not an instance of the argument "from the less to the greater" (kal vehomer)? If David, king of Israel who learned from Ahitophel no more than two things, nevertheless called him his master, his guide and his beloved friend; then in the case of one who learns from his fellow one chapter, or one halakhah, or one verse, or one word, or even one letter, all the more so he is under obligation to treat him with honor. And "honor'" means nothing but Torah, as it is said[7], "It is honor that sages inherit". "And[8] the perfect shall inherit

---

[3] Proverbs 11:22
[4] Exodus 32:16
[5] Numbers 21:19
[6] Psalms 55:14
[7] Proverbs 3:35
[8] Proverbs 28:10

good", and "good" means nothing but Torah, as it is said[9], "For I give you good instruction; do not forsake my Torah".

4. Such is the way of a life of Torah: you shall eat bread with salt, and rationed water shall you drink; you shall sleep on the ground, your life will be one of privation, and in Torah shall you labor. If you do this[10], "Happy shall you be and it shall be good for you": "Happy shall you be" in this world, "and it shall be good for you" in the world to come.

5. Do not seek greatness for yourself, and do not covet honor. Practice more than you learn. Do not yearn for the table of kings, for your table is greater than their table, and your crown is greater than their crown, and faithful is your employer to pay you the reward of your labor.

6. Greater is learning Torah than the priesthood and than royalty, for royalty is acquired by thirty stages, and the priesthood by twenty-four, but the Torah by forty-eight things. By study, Attentive listening, Proper speech, By an understanding heart, By an intelligent heart, By awe, By fear, By humility, By joy, By attending to the sages, By critical give and take with friends, By fine argumentation with disciples, By clear thinking, By study of Scripture, By study of mishnah, By a minimum of sleep, By a minimum of chatter, By a minimum of pleasure, By a minimum of frivolity, By a minimum of preoccupation with worldly matters, By long-suffering, By generosity, By faith in the sages, By acceptance of suffering. Learning of Torah is also

---

[9] Proverbs 4:2
[10] Psalms 128:2

acquired by one Who recognizes his place, Who rejoices in his portion, Who makes a fence about his words, Who takes no credit for himself, Who is loved, Who loves God, Who loves his fellow creatures, Who loves righteous ways, Who loves reproof, Who loves uprightness, Who keeps himself far from honors, Who does not let his heart become swelled on account of his learning, Who does not delight in giving legal decisions, Who shares in the bearing of a burden with his colleague, Who judges with the scales weighted in his favor, Who leads him on to truth, Who leads him on to peace, Who composes himself at his study, Who asks and answers, Who listens to others, and himself adds to his knowledge, Who learns in order to teach, Who learns in order to practice, Who makes his teacher wiser, Who is exact in what he has learned, And who says a thing in the name of him who said it. Thus, you have learned: everyone who says a thing in the name of him who said it, brings deliverance into the world, as it is said[11]: "And Esther told the king in Mordecai's name".

7. Great is Torah for it gives life to those that practice it, in this world, and in the world to come, As it is said[12]: "For they are life unto those that find them, and health to all their flesh", And it says[13]: "It will be a cure for your navel and marrow for your bones", And it says[14]: "She is a tree of life to those that grasp her, and whoever

---

[11] Esther 2:22
[12] Proverbs 4:22
[13] Proverbs 3:8
[14] Proverbs 3:18

holds onto her is happy", And it says[15]: "For they are a graceful wreath upon your head, a necklace about your throat", And it says[16]: "She will adorn your head with a graceful wreath; crown you with a glorious diadem". And it says[17]: "In her right hand is length of days, in her left riches and honor", And it says[18]: "For they will bestow on you length of days, years of life and peace".

8. Rabbi Shimon ben Menasya said in the name of Rabbi Shimon ben Yohai: Beauty, strength, riches, honor, wisdom, old age, gray hair, and children are becoming to the righteous, and becoming to the world, As it is said[19]: "Gray hair is a crown of glory (beauty); it is attained by way of righteousness", And it says[20]: "The ornament of the wise is their wealth", And it says[21]: "The glory of youths is their strength; and the beauty of old men is their gray hair", And it says[22]: "Grandchildren are the glory of their elders, and the glory of children is their parents", And it says[23]: "Then the moon shall be ashamed, and the sun shall be abashed. For the Lord of Hosts will reign on Mount Zion and in Jerusalem, and God's Honor will be revealed to his elders". Rabbi Shimon ben Menasya said: these seven qualities, which the sages have listed

---

[15] Proverbs 1:9
[16] Proverbs 4:9
[17] Proverbs 3:1
[18] Proverbs 3:2
[19] Proverbs 16:31
[20] Proverbs 14:24
[21] Proverbs 20:29
[22] Proverbs 17:6
[23] Isaiah 24:23

as becoming to the righteous, were all of them fulfilled in Rabbi and his sons.

9. Rabbi Yose ben Kisma said: Once I was walking by the way when a man met me, and greeted me and I greeted him. He said to me, "Rabbi, where are you from?" I said to him, "I am from a great city of sages and scribes". He said to me, "Rabbi, would you consider living with us in our place? I would give you a thousand thousand denarii of gold, and precious stones and pearls." I said to him: "My son, even if you were to give me all the silver and gold, precious stones and pearls that are in the world, I would not dwell anywhere except in a place of Torah; for when a man passes away there accompany him neither gold nor silver, nor precious stones nor pearls, but Torah and good deeds alone, as it is said[24], "When you walk it will lead you. When you lie down it will watch over you; and when you are awake it will talk with you". "When you walk it will lead you" in this world. "When you lie down it will watch over you" in the grave; "And when you are awake it will talk with you" in the world to come. And thus, it is written in the book of Psalms by David, king of Israel[25], "I prefer the teaching You proclaimed to thousands of pieces of gold and silver", And it says[26]: "Mine is the silver, and mine the gold, says the Lord of Hosts".

10. Five possessions did the Holy Blessed One, set aside as his own in this world, and these are they: The Torah, one possession; Heaven and earth, another

---

[24] Proverbs 6:22
[25] Psalms 119:72
[26] Haggai 2:8

possession; Abraham, another possession; Israel, another possession; The Temple, another possession.

A. The Torah is one possession. From where do we know this? Since it is written[27], "The Lord possessed (usually translated as 'created') me at the beginning of his course, at the first of His works of old".

B. Heaven and earth, another possession. From where do we know this? Since it is said[28]: "Thus said the Lord: The heaven is My throne and the earth are My footstool; Where could you build a house for Me, what place could serve as My abode? And it says[29]: "How many are the things You have made, O Lord; You have made them all with wisdom; the earth is full of Your possessions".

C. Abraham is another possession. From where do we know this? Since it is written[30]: "He blessed him, saying, "Blessed by Abram of God Most High, Possessor of heaven and earth".

D. Israel is another possession. From where do we know this? Since it is written[31]: "Till Your people cross over, O Lord, Till Your people whom You have possessed". And it says[32]: "As to the holy and mighty ones that are in the land, my whole desire (possession) is in them".

E. The Temple is another possession. From where do we know this? Since it is said[33]: "The sanctuary, O lord,

---

[27] Proverbs 8:22
[28] Isaiah 66:1
[29] Psalms 104:24
[30] Genesis 15:19
[31] Exodus 15:16
[32] Psalms 16:3
[33] Exodus 15:17

which your hands have established". And it says[34]: "And He brought them to His holy realm, to the mountain, which His right hand had possessed".

11. Whatever the Holy Blessed One created in His world, he created only for His glory, as it is said[35]: "All who are linked to My name, whom I have created, formed and made for My glory", And it says[36]: "The Lord shall reign for ever and ever".

12. Said Rabbi Hananiah ben Akashya: It pleased the Holy Blessed One to grant merit to Israel, that is why He gave them Torah and commandments in abundance, as it is said[37], "The Lord was pleased for His righteousness, to make Torah great and glorious".

---

[34] Psalms 78:54
[35] Isaiah 43:7
[36] Exodus 15:18
[37] Isaiah 42:21

PIRKI AVOT   Chapter 6   Rambam

www.ingramcontent.com/pod-product-compliance
Lightning Source LLC
Chambersburg PA
CBHW070155080526
44586CB00015B/1994